# THE BUFFALO SOLDIERS

Frederic Remington.
San Carlos. Arizona.

AFRICAN-AMERICAN ACHIEVERS

# THE BUFFALO SOLDIERS

*TaRessa Stovall*

*CHELSEA HOUSE PUBLISHERS*
*Philadelphia*

**Chelsea House Publishers**
*Editor-in-Chief* Stephen Reginald
*Managing Editor* James D. Gallagher
*Production Manager* Pamela Loos
*Art Director* Sara Davis
*Picture Editor* Judy Hasday
*Senior Production Editor* Lisa Chippendale

**Staff for THE BUFFALO SOLDIERS**
*Design and Typography* Duke & Company
*Picture Researcher* Alan Gottlieb, Sandy Jones
*Cover Design/Illustration* Robert Gerson

First Printing

1 3 5 7 9 8 6 4 2

Library of Congress Cataloging-in-Publication Data

Stovall, TaRessa.
The Buffalo Soldiers/TaRessa Stovall.

   p. cm. —(African-American Achievers)
Includes bibliographical references and index.
Summary: An account of the achievements of the Afro-American Army regiments that distinguished
themselves during the numerous campaigns and played a vital role in the settlement of the American West.

ISBN     0-7910-2595-0 (hc.)
ISBN     0-7910-2596-9 (pbk.)

1. Afro-Americans—West (U.S.)—History—19th century—Juvenile literature. 2. Afro-American soldiers
—West (U.S.)—History—19th century—Juvenile literature. 3. United States Army—Afro-American
troops—History—19th century—Juvenile literature. 4. Frontier and pioneer life—West (U.S.)—Juvenile
literature. 5. United States. Army. Cavalry, 10th—Juvenile literature. 6. United States. Army. Cavalry,
9th—Juvenile literature. 7. Indians of North America—Wars—1860–1890—Juvenile literature.
[1. Afro-Americans—History—19th century. 2. Afro-American soldiers—History—19th century.
3. United States. Army. —Afro-American troops. 4. Frontier and pioneer life—West (U.S.) 5. United
States. Army. Cavalry, 10th. 6. United States. Army. Cavalry, 9th. 7. Indians of North America—Wars—
1866–1895. 8. West (U.S.)—History—1860–1890.] I. Title. II. Series.
E185.925S76  1997
978′.00496073—dc21

                                                                                    97-14568
                                                                                         CIP
                                                                                          AC

Frontispiece: *A Buffalo Soldier guards his post on the frontier in this 1888
painting, "The Alert," by Frederic Remington.*
On the cover: *Troop E, 9th U.S. Cavalry en route to the Philippines, 1900.*
Cover photo credit: *Courtesy U.S. Army Military History Institute.*

# CONTENTS

**1**
The Freedom to Fight   9

**2**
Westward Bound   21

**3**
In Search of Chief Victorio   31

**4**
The Fight for Equality   43

**5**
On the Frontier   51

**6**
To Cuba   63

**7**
In the Trenches   73

**8**
Continuing Courage   85

Chronology   96

Further Reading   98

Index   100

# AFRICAN-AMERICAN ACHIEVERS

THE BLACK COWBOYS

THE BLACK MUSLIMS

BOYZ II MEN

THE BUFFALO SOLDIERS

THE HARLEM GLOBETROTTERS

THE HARLEM RENAISSANCE

THE NEGRO LEAGUES

THE TEMPTATIONS

# THE BUFFALO SOLDIERS

# 1

# The Freedom to Fight

By 1864 Abraham Lincoln, who had first thought that providing arms to black men would only result in them surrendering them to their former masters, had concluded that black soldiers "have demonstrated in their blood the right to the ballot." In the years following Lincoln's assassination, black men gained, then quickly lost, the ballot, but they did win a permanent right to serve in the U.S. Army.

—William Loren Katz
The Black West

ON JULY 28, 1866, the United States Congress approved the enlistment of Negro soldiers in the peacetime U.S. Army. This led to the formation of the 9th and 10th Colored Cavalry (horseback) units and the 38th, 39th, 40th, and 41st Infantry (foot soldier) units, the first black military troops to serve during peacetime.

When the soldiers of the new Colored Cavalries first fell into formation, they stood tall and straight, proud to serve their country. They had high hopes that this might be a step toward the equality that African Americans had been denied for so long, but true freedom, they were to learn, would be a long time coming, and some of the most challenging battles lay ahead.

These were not the first African Americans to fight for their country. African Americans had defended

*Many African Americans proudly served in their country's military long before receiving the full benefits of citizenship in the United States. This young soldier was one of 180,000 black soldiers who helped the Union cause during the Civil War.*

*Crispus Attucks, a former slave, was one of the earliest American patriots. He was killed by British troops in what became known as the "Boston Massacre."*

the United States and died for it long before the nation considered them full-fledged soldiers or granted them the rights of full citizens. Black involvement in American warfare dates at least to the 1770s and the period of the Revolutionary War.

On March 5, 1770, for example, Crispus Attucks, a former slave, led a group of protesters through Boston to defy armed British troops. Attucks died when British soldiers fired into the crowd in what came to be known as the "Boston Massacre." Some historical accounts also mention Peter Salem, an African-American man who took part in the first major battle of the Revolutionary War, the Battle of Bunker Hill. Salem shot and killed a British officer during that battle, which took place on June 17, 1775.

American military history includes other examples of black men fighting for their country. By the start of the War of 1812, a war waged between the United States and Great Britain, nearly one-fifth of the U.S. Navy was African American. Among the black sailors was John Johnson. A British bullet fatally injured Johnson during the Battle of Lake Erie, a battle that ended with an American victory. Johnson is said to have spent the last moments of his life encouraging his shipmates to keep up the fight. The ship's commander, Nathan Shaler, later urged his men to remember Johnson "with reverence as long as bravery is considered a virtue." Black soldiers also took part in the Battle of New Orleans, the final battle in the War of 1812. The victorious Americans came out of that battle with 71 dead, while the British suffered 2,500 casualties.

Despite their contributions to America's military successes in the Revolutionary War and the War of 1812, African Americans were unwelcome participants as far as the federal government was concerned. A 1792 law stated that only "free able-bodied white males" were to serve in the U.S. Armed Forces. In 1798, the Secretary of War ordered that "no Negro, mulatto [a person of mixed black and white heritage] or Indian is to be enlisted" in the Marine Corps. The federal government later issued another policy statement which maintained, "No Negro will be received as a recruit of the Army."

The turning point for black Americans in the military came during the Civil War. When the war broke out, many blacks longed to wear the North's union blue and fight for their freedom. However, according to the *Journal of Negro History*, black soldiers discovered that "their services were neither wanted at that time nor contemplated in the future." Many northern whites thought the Civil War would be brief. As the war dragged on and casualties rose, however, the federal government asked blacks to fight against the South and against slavery.

African-American historian Walter Dean Myers explains in *Now Is Your Time! The African American Struggle For Freedom* that "the North had resisted us-

*In 1862, President Abraham Lincoln (left) signed the Emancipation Proclamation, which ended slavery, and removed a ban on blacks in the military. Despite resistance from some officers, General Ulysses S. Grant (right) integrated all-black regiments into the Union Army.*

ing Africans as soldiers. Some whites said that the Africans . . . were too accustomed to being dominated by white men to fight them; others thought Africans weren't agile enough to fight. But the North needed fresh troops and so a plan was developed to accept Africans into the Union Army."

The Emancipation Proclamation of 1862 called for an end to slavery and reversed the ban on blacks in the military. This opened the way for their enlistment in the Union Army, mainly as laborers. Thousands joined the black regiments of the U.S. Army. Because whites believed that blacks could serve but not lead, the black troops were all commanded by white officers. While a few Negro soldiers did become officers during the Civil War, they were not allowed to command troops.

Some white officers opposed the idea of having black soldiers under their command. General Ulysses S. Grant, commander of the Union forces, was unsympathetic to their views. He reminded his officers: "It is expected that all commanders will especially exert themselves in carrying out the policy of the administration, not only in organizing colored regiments and rendering them effective, but also in removing prejudice against them."

Still, many white officers resented being asked to serve with Negro troops and threatened to leave. After warnings that those who deserted would be shot, attitudes began to change. Acceptance of an integrated army slowly grew as the black troops distinguished themselves as courageous and skillful soldiers. On September 29, 1864, for example, Northern regiments marched toward the southern town of New Market Heights, Virginia. The Union force included nine regiments of black troops. Confederate soldiers fiercely defended the town, killing many Union soldiers, but the Union soldiers rallied and captured New Market Heights within a day. Benjamin Butler, the commanding Union general, commended the efforts of the black troops, saying, "I felt in my inmost heart that the capacity of the Negro race for soldiers had then and there been fully satisfied forever."

The all-black 54th Massachusetts Infantry regiment also distinguished itself during the Civil War. The 54th led a now-famous attack on Fort Wagner, South Carolina, the night of July 18, 1863, charging through a hail of enemy gunfire to breach the walls of the fort. Sergeant William Carney braved gunshot wounds to carry the Union flag proudly to the front of the battle lines, and he became the first African American to receive the Congressional Medal of Honor for bravery in battle. Lewis Douglass, a soldier in the 54th, wrote that "not a man flinched, though it was a trying time."

Black soldiers fought bravely in battles at Milliken's Bend, Louisiana; Baxter Springs, Kansas; and Point Lookout, Virginia. Hundreds were ambushed at Fort Pillow, Tennessee. The legacy of skilled fighting and outstanding courage was one of which black Civil War soldiers could be proud.

Some 180,000 black men fought in the Civil War,

and 33,380 gave their lives. Black women made their contribution as laborers, guides, nurses, and spies. With that conflict behind them, many African Americans looked for other opportunities to serve and defend their country. The U.S. government helped to make this possible with a law enacted on July 28, 1866. The new law allowed Negroes to serve in the regular peacetime army. Four black infantry and cavalry units were formed. In early August 1866, the 9th and 10th Colored Cavalry regiments, which would become known as the Buffalo Soldiers, were established.

The 9th Cavalry, led by Civil War hero Edward Hatch, was organized at Greenville, Louisiana. The 10th, led by distinguished cavalryman Benjamin Grierson, was formed at Fort Leavenworth, Kansas. The white commanding officers and their black troops joined forces only to find that their first battles would be with each other and the U.S. Army they had committed to serve.

Having Negro troops in the peacetime army was such a radical change that the military had to develop new rules. Each regiment was assigned a chaplain to teach the soldiers reading, writing, and math, and to provide spiritual guidance. The officers, all of whom were white, had to have served two years of active field service in the Civil War and were required to pass a special exam given by a group of veteran officers.

It was difficult to find good officers to lead the Negro regiments. Grierson and Hatch had several hundred recruits, along with arms and horses, but no officers to lead them. Many white officers were so convinced that blacks could never be good soldiers that they took a lower rank to serve with a white regiment. For example, one advertisement at this time in the *Army and Navy Journal* stated:

> A first Lieutenant of Infantry stationed at a very desirable post in the Department of the South desires a transfer with an officer of the same grade, on *equal* terms if in a white regiment; but if in a colored regiment, a reasonable bonus would be expected.

*Colonel Benjamin Grierson commanded the 10th Cavalry—the original "Buffalo Soldiers"—for 22 years. However, finding other good officers to lead the Negro regiments was difficult.*

Black men from all over the South enlisted in the army. Many had been farmers, truck drivers, cooks, bakers, servants, and cigar makers. They were hungry for adventure, opportunity, food, shelter, clothing, regular pay, and a new way of life. Slavery had only recently ended, and even for skilled black men, a military career was one of the few options available. The salary of $13 a month was more than they could earn as civilians, and with clothing, shelter, and food included, it was the best opportunity most black men had seen in their lifetimes. As William Loren Katz noted in *The Black West*, "In an age that viewed black men as either comic or dangerous, and steadily reduced the decent jobs open to them, army life offered more dignity that almost anything civilian life had to offer."

Once enlisted, black soldiers worked hard at their jobs—as much out of personal pride as necessity. "Because economic options for blacks were so limited during the late 1880s, the Buffalo Soldiers saw military service as a privilege and an honor," Pierre Hauser writes in *The Community Builders*. "As a result, they applied themselves to their Army duties more enthusi-

*Members of the 10th Cavalry outside their guardhouse. In 1867, the newly formed 9th and 10th Cavalries were sent to the frontier.*

astically than their white colleagues; they deserted less often; received fewer courts-martial, and kept themselves in better physical condition. These qualities drew them high praise from their white commanders and other observers."

The black regiments faced many difficulties that white soldiers and officers never encountered. Even those men with war experience needed additional training to become professional soldiers. Few of the blacks could read or write, and many had beliefs that the white officers considered backward and superstitious.

The commander of Fort Leavenworth, General William Hoffman, did everything in his power to make life miserable for Grierson and the Negro troops of

the 10th Cavalry. He gave them old, decrepit weapons and broken-down horses, and assigned them to swampy quarters, which caused many of the men to develop pneumonia. Hoffman refused Grierson's requests for dry walkways and better quarters. Captain Louis Carpenter, a white officer of the 10th Cavalry, complained that even the flag given to his regiment was faded and worn compared to the silk-embroidered flags routinely handed out to white regiments.

In the face of these obstacles, Grierson struggled to work his recruits into shape. He set high standards for his men and instructed army recruiters to send him "men sufficiently educated to fill the positions of Non-Commissioned Officers, clerks and mechanics in this regiment. You will use the greatest care in your selection of recruits . . . enlist all the superior men . . . who will be a credit to the regiment."

Grierson's standards were so high that by September 1866, he had only one Negro soldier, Private William Beauman, and he was sick with malaria. As winter approached, more recruits and officers began arriving. Grierson assigned them to find more soldiers. Rather than scouting the southern states, he instructed them to search in northern cities such as Philadelphia, New York, Pittsburgh, and Boston.

A perfectionist, Grierson was strict with careless officers. After he informed a recruiter, Captain H. T. Davis, "You will have to foot the bill for your rejects in the future," he began getting better recruits. Still, at the beginning of 1867, he had only seven officers and 80 soldiers. Many more came in the spring, which caused greater tension between Grierson and Hoffman, who openly looked down on the Negro soldiers and the officers who led them.

Grierson constantly protested the unequal treatment of his soldiers, demanding better weapons, horses, and living quarters. He told the officers who reported to him that they were not to "refer to this regiment as the 10th *Colored* Cavalry, but as the 10th Cavalry. Regardless of their colored skins, they are soldiers of the U.S. Army."

In return, Hoffman harassed Grierson, ordering black troops to stay at least 10 yards from white troops and refusing to let black soldiers march in review. As he struggled to lift his troops' morale, Grierson maintained his vision. "Colored troops will hold their place in the Army of the United States as long as the government lasts," he wrote in a letter.

Grierson faced yet another battle—the struggle to get good, strong horses for his troops. The oldest, most crippled animals—many left over from the Civil War—were assigned to the Negro regiments. Grierson fought for years to improve this situation.

In Greenville, Louisiana, the commander of the 9th Cavalry, Edward Hatch, also faced challenges. He had plenty of Negro soldiers and a good number of white officers, but there was not much for them to do, so they gambled, drank, and fought. Many men became sick from the crowded quarters and poorly cooked food. Twenty-three died from cholera and some deserted in fear for their lives.

By February 1867 Hatch had assembled 12 companies, and in March they were transferred to Brownsville and San Antonio, Texas. However, Hatch's men were disorganized, rowdy, and unprepared for the move. One company threatened to desert on its way to San Antonio. Tensions, fueled by racism and frustration, flared between the citizens of San Antonio and the soldiers who were protecting them. The troops clashed with the police, and in a mutiny attempt on April 9, an officer and two troopers were shot.

This time, when Hatch asked the War Department for better officers, he got them quickly and conditions improved. In May, Hatch was ordered to move the 9th Cavalry west to Fort Stockton and Fort Davis in Texas to guard hundreds of miles of wild frontier.

In August, Grierson was told to move the 10th Cavalry from Fort Leavenworth to Fort Riley, Kansas, where conditions and relations with the commanding officer were much improved. Once he reached Fort Riley, Grierson was joined by Lieutenant Samuel Woodward, a friend from the Civil War. For 20 years, "Sandy" Woodward led the 10th Cavalry under Grierson's command.

At the end of their first year, the 9th and 10th Cavalries were growing and becoming better organized, although it still was not clear how they would perform in battle. In the spring and summer of 1867, both cavalries began moving westward. The move marked a beginning for the Buffalo Soldiers. For here, on the Great Plains and in the New Mexico and Arizona deserts and mountains, they would make a name for themselves.

A CAMPFIRE SKETCH.

# 2

# Westward Bound

THE 10TH CAVALRY rode westward from Kansas throughout the summer and fall of 1867. They were headed toward lands that were home to the Cheyenne, Arapaho, Crow, Shoshone, and Lakota (Sioux). The ranks of the 10th Cavalry included former laborers, farmers, soldiers, sailors, cooks, and barbers. Some, like Civil War veteran George Washington Williams of Pennsylvania, had grown bored with the routine of civilian life after the war. Williams joined the 10th Cavalry because he longed "for the outdoor, lively, exhilarating exercise of military life." Others, like 19-year-old George Jordan of Kentucky, had no military experience. The men of the 10th ranged in age from 18 to 35 and had differing backgrounds, but many shared the sentiments expressed by one black youth who said that he joined the cavalry because "I got tired of looking mules in the face from sunrise to sunset. Thought there must be a better livin' in this world."

At the same time, the 9th Cavalry headed for western and southwestern Texas, home of the Comanche and their allies, the Kiowa. The men of the 9th Cavalry hailed from many states, with a large number coming from Louisiana and Kentucky. Their ages ranged from 18 to 34. Among them was Civil War vet-

*Western artist Frederic Remington sketched these members of the 10th Cavalry around a campfire.*

eran Jacob Wilks, whose parents escaped slavery while he was still a baby. His fellow soldiers in the 9th Cavalry included farmers, laborers, and other Civil War veterans, many of whom had once been slaves.

Even those soldiers in the 9th and 10th Cavalries who had never been slaves had experienced racial prejudice. Although racism was not absent from the military, many of the black soldiers found in the army the freedom and opportunities that had eluded them at home in post–Civil War America. Their search for a better life came with a price, though, for the 9th and 10th Cavalries stood at the center of the United States' conquest of Native American lands reaching all the way to the Great Plains. "In that vast land, men of two outcast races met in battle on desert, plain, and mountain for over twenty years, while a government that hated them both imposed white domination over them and their people," author Clinton Cox writes in *The Forgotten Heroes: The Story of the Buffalo Soldiers.*

However, the Buffalo Soldiers met their duties with integrity and honor. They performed numerous acts of heroism during more than 20 years of continuous service in the West.

The men of the 9th and 10th Cavalries made up 20 percent of the U.S. Cavalry in the western states. Although much of their time was spent battling the Indians, they also had many other duties. Civil authorities often called on the army to help establish some form of law and order. The soldiers of the 9th and 10th Cavalries joined in those efforts, helping to control the lawless actions of cattle thieves, murderous politicians, greedy land and cattle barons, crooked government contractors, and heartless Indian agents. In addition, the black cavalries protected railroad crews, escorted stagecoaches and trains, and scouted in the region.

By August 1867, when the Buffalo Soldiers began arriving in the West, war had already come to the Central and Southern Plains. Cheyenne, Arapaho, and

Sioux tribes, upset at being forced off their homelands by white settlers, joined forces and nearly stopped work on the growing Kansas Pacific Railroad line. White soldiers, teamsters, trappers, and travelers were attacked. Tensions flared and casualties mounted on both sides. On the Texas frontier, the Kiowa and Comanche tribes wounded, captured, and killed dozens of settlers and stole thousands of horses and cattle. Captain E. L. Smith in Fort Arbuckle called for a thousand men to quiet the rebellions.

Three companies of the 10th Cavalry, 34 soldiers in all, were sent to the Indian territories, while the other nine companies were stationed at camps and posts on the Santa Fe and Smoky Hill railroad lines. Shortly after beginning their journey, the soldiers of the 10th were surrounded by armed Cheyennes, who fired at them from behind rocks and shrubs. The soldiers fought, trapped in place under the burning sun,

*In 1867, the 9th Cavalry was sent to Texas, which was occupied by Comanche and Kiowa tribes. The Native Americans admired the soldiers' fighting ability and nicknamed them "Buffalo Soldiers."*

*Troopers of the 10th Cavalry take a break on the trail. The Buffalo Soldiers made up 20 percent of the U.S. Cavalry serving in the western states.*

for six hours. Then, nearly out of bullets, they tried a desperate and daring maneuver: shooting their way past the surrounding Indians. The Cheyennes chased them for 15 miles, but 33 soldiers escaped. Sergeant William Christy, a farmer from Pennsylvania, took a bullet to the head and became the 10th Cavalry's first battlefield casualty.

The Native Americans apparently admired the African-American soldiers' courage and fighting ability, and they began calling them "Buffalo Soldiers." Some say that the black soldiers' curly black hair reminded the Indians of a buffalo's tightly coiled fur. In any case, the new name was quickly and enthusiastically accepted first by the men of the 10th Cavalry, and later by the men of the 9th Cavalry. Recognizing that the buffalo was a sacred animal to the Indian,

and that only a respected enemy would be named for it, they proudly called themselves the Buffalo Soldiers and featured a buffalo in their regimental crest. The pride associated with the term was so strong that all of the racially segregated black American ground units from 1866 to 1950 called themselves Buffalo Soldiers.

The 9th Cavalry left Fort McKavett, Texas, to hunt for a band of Apache who had been fighting with settlers. After weeks of searching, their clothing tattered and their boots torn, the Buffalo Soldiers found the Apaches, who outnumbered the soldiers and began an armed attack from behind. The soldiers were ordered to turn around and ride toward the Apaches.

Emanuel Stance of South Carolina became the first to put his life on the line when he led the group forward, ordering them to fire. Overwhelmed, the

*The treaties of Medicine Lodge were intended to stop fighting between Native Americans and white settlers. However, the U.S. government broke many of its promises, and the Buffalo Soldiers were ordered to quell the fighting that resulted.*

Apaches retreated. Stance later received the Congressional Medal of Honor, making him the first of 20 soldiers from the 9th and 10th Cavalries to receive that award. He wrote that he would "cherish the gift as a thing of priceless value and endeavor by my future conduct to merit the high honor conferred upon me."

Other than Stance, however, few Buffalo Soldiers who fought in the Indian Wars were ever thanked or rewarded for their efforts. Major Guy Henry, one of the white officers of the 9th Cavalry, described fighting in the Indian Wars as dangerous because the foe is behind cover; difficult due to reduced rations, bitter cold, rules against building fires, and a lack of transportation or care for the wounded and sick; and thankless because, as Henry stated, "the sense of duty performed in defense of the weak settler is your only reward."

By the winter of 1867–68, the U.S. government's Indian Peace Commission and several tribes had signed treaties creating permanent reservations far from the roads and railroads being built all across the west. The Comanche, Kiowa, and Kiowa-Apache agreed to move to a reservation of about three million acres between the Washita and Red Rivers. The Cheyenne and Arapaho got more than four million acres to the north. The Indians were promised all of the food, clothing, and supplies they needed, as well as the right to hunt buffalo south of the Arkansas River. In exchange, the Indians were to stop fighting, leave the whites alone, and stay away from the main roads.

These treaties, known as the treaties of Medicine Lodge, stopped the wars on the Central Plains, but not all tribes had taken part in the talks or agreed to the government's terms. In the southern part of the region, groups of Kiowa and Comanche continued to harass settlers and other Indian tribes. Nevertheless, Grierson decided the peace was firm enough to move most of his men to Fort Riley for the winter, leaving only a few behind to guard railroad camps along the Kansas Pacific Railway.

Hopes for a winter spent far from Indian territory were dashed almost as soon as the first soldiers arrived at Fort Riley. Some were sent to Fort Gibson, near the northern end of the Cheyenne-Arapaho reservation. Others were transferred to Fort Arbuckle, near the southern part of the Cheyenne-Araphaho reservation. At Fort Arbuckle, the Buffalo Soldiers' work included enlarging the fort. As it turned out, their biggest enemies that winter, Clinton Cox writes, "were boredom, whiskey bootleggers, cattle rustlers, outlaws, and the racial prejudice that remained with them throughout their careers."

Boredom was an especially big problem. The men had little to do but huddle close to the stoves in their barracks on cold winter nights. Desertion rates among the Buffalo Soldiers, which had not been high previously, rose. Many young recruits fled, and some died as they struck out across the inhospitable winter prairie.

Unrest among the Native Americans who had not signed the Medicine Lodge treaties, and non-Indians who acted as though the agreements never existed, created new duties for the black soldiers. Many spent the winter tracking down hunters who violated the treaties by killing thousands of buffalo and selling their hides for profit. Others took on the job of delivering the mail. Mail carriers were being murdered so often on their runs between Fort Arbuckle and Fort Gibson that eventually white soldiers refused to do the job, and teams of Indian scouts were formed to deliver the mail. Individual Buffalo Soldiers, who often in their careers took on hazardous work that others refused to perform, also began delivering the mail.

Private Filmore Roberts, a 21-year-old laborer from Iowa, was one of those assigned to take the mail from Fort Arbuckle to Fort Gibson in the middle of winter. When he failed to arrive, his name was added to the list of deserters. Months later, the remains of his body were discovered near the Canadian River, the mail pouch strapped to his back. He had lost his life trying to cross the swollen stream to deliver the mail to the fort.

Congress's failure to deliver on the peace commission's promises of food, blankets, and other essentials desperately needed by those Indians who had moved to the reservations further threatened the peace. In frustration, many warriors left the reservations and resumed their attacks on white settlers. They also attacked other Indian bands, especially those who had taken up farming and adopted other aspects of white culture. As Cox explains:

> Now, with hunger stalking the reservations, anger came quickly to men who had only reluctantly agreed to the peace terms at Medicine Lodge. They watched their wives and children grow thinner, and they felt betrayed. And so they lashed out at those around them who possessed the land they had once lived on and who possessed food while the warriors and those they loved went hungry.

The job of quelling the violence among Native Americans and staving off the threat of open warfare between Native Americans and whites fell to the Buffalo Soldiers. Their work was complicated by continued government inaction. When the government finally delivered some of the food promised by the treaties, it consisted of salt pork, moldy cornmeal, and flour contaminated by mouse droppings. Many Native Americans chiefs who had, until this point, managed to contain the anger and frustration mounting around them no longer tried to do so. Violence flared in northwestern Kansas, where Indians killed and wounded forty white settlers.

One group of Buffalo Soldiers was ordered to search for the attackers while another group was sent to protect a stage coach route that had endured numerous attacks. Other groups of Buffalo Soldiers fanned out across the plains to protect besieged settlers. By the end of the summer of 1868, the Buffalo Soldiers of the 9th and 10th Cavalries had covered thousands of miles of territory from Kansas to the Texas-Mexico border in their efforts to protect the settlers and hold together the fragile peace. A great deal more work lay ahead.

# 3

# In Search of Chief Victorio

*The Ninth marched out with splendid cheer,*
*The Bad Lands to explore*
*With Colonel Henry at their head*
*They never fear the foe;*

*So on they rode from Christmas eve;*
*'Til dawn of Christmas day;*
*The Red Skins heard the Ninth was near*
*and fled in great dismay.*

—Ballad penned by a Buffalo Soldier

ONE OF THE Buffalo Soldiers' greatest challenges was the long, frustrating hunt for Chief Victorio, a fearless warrior and leader of the Warm Springs (Ojo Caliente) Apache. Victorio, known as the Apache Wolf, was a forceful and cunning leader. In 1875, his people had agreed to live on a reservation in a mountainous, tree-filled region of New Mexico—land that had been home to them for many years. A year later, however, speculators pressed the U.S. government to remove the Apache so that they could divert the area's plentiful water and timber supplies to the growing town of Tucson nearby. Despite warnings that such a move would lead to war, the government agreed and the Apache were forced to leave. They were relocated to the dry, barren San Carlos Reservations in eastern Arizona. Victorio and another Apache chief, Geron-

*Apache Chief Victorio was a cunning leader who refused to be removed from his homeland and confined to a reservation. Known as the Apache Wolf, he led a war against the U.S. for five years. Both the 9th and 10th Cavalries were involved in the fight against Victorio.*

*Buffalo Soldiers of the 10th Cavalry make camp during the Apache campaign.*

imo, were arrested and carted in wagons to San Carlos in shackles. Victorio did not remain there for long.

In September 1877, three hundred Apaches escaped from San Carlos, led by Chief Victorio. They traveled throughout the land, killing anyone who crossed their path. The government wanted Victorio—dead or alive. The 9th Cavalry was called to find him.

Colonel Hatch's soldiers tracked Victorio and his men into the treacherous Mogollon mountains, one step behind the renegade Indians. The Apaches had left the reservation in a rush, taking little food, clothing, or ammunition. With winter approaching and many of his followers barefoot, naked, and hungry, Victorio decided to surrender. Nearly two hundred Apaches, led by their proud chief, arrived at Fort Wingate in October. A few days later, 70 other Apaches joined them.

William Leckie relates part of the story in his book,

*The Buffalo Soldiers: A Narrative of the Negro Cavalry in the West:*

> Victorio told [the commanding officer] at Wingate that he and his people would not willingly return to San Carlos; that they preferred to return to Warm Springs, and that this was the place they wished to be buried. For a time it appeared that this wish might be granted, and escorted by Companies I and L of the 9th, they were taken to Warm Springs [without any] arms and horses. But their stay was a short one and before October was out they were back at San Carlos once more, although eighty of them, including Victorio, had managed to escape while en route.

In early 1878, Victorio and some of his men again surrendered, this time at Warm Springs. They told the authorities that they would stay in their old homes but would not consider going back to San Carlos. Government agents decided to send them instead to the Mescalero reservation to rejoin other members of the tribe. Dissatisfied, the Apaches fled. A few months later, they returned to the Mescalero reservation and received promises of better treatment from the government. Their wives and children were brought from San Carlos to Mescalero, and for a while it seemed as though peace had arrived. Instead of chasing Victorio's Apaches, the soldiers of the 9th Cavalry spent their days protecting them from roving gangs of white outlaws who saw the Indians on the reservation as easy targets.

Although all was quiet for a time, the Apaches still resented the fact that they had been forced from their beloved homeland to a reservation where they had no rights and were given little, if any, respect. Tension grew when a judge and prosecuting attorney arrived at the reservation. Fearing arrest on old charges of horse stealing and murder, Victorio fled. "He hid in the mountains of Mexico and began to recruit warriors, vowing to 'make war forever' on the United States," Clinton Cox writes.

Victorio's war began at Ojo Caliente, where members of the 9th Cavalry were stationed. However, the Apache chief was not their only foe; long-simmering racial problems between the black soldiers of Company E and their white commanding officer surfaced at a most unfortunate time. It was the opening Victorio needed. In September 1879, Victorio and his warriors attacked Company E, killing eight soldiers and running off 46 of their 50 horses. The soldiers blamed the deaths on their commanding officer, a man who had for years made derogatory comments about the black soldiers under his command. The commander, Captain Theodore Hooker, had refused to increase the number of men on guard even after the company received word of Victorio's presence in the area. After the raid, according to the other soldiers, Hooker commented that he wished all of his men had been killed.

The Apaches continued their rampage, murdering nine whites, and Colonel Hatch put his men on the search. The 9th Cavalry hunted Victorio for months, struggling over rough, rocky lands. The soldiers made long night marches on foot, trying to surprise the Indians in their camps. Colonel Hatch wrote of the difficult mission:

> the work performed by these troops is most arduous, horses worn to mere shadows, men nearly without boots, shoes and clothing. . . . We always fight in extended skirmish line, the Indian line is always found to be of the same length and often longer, extending in some actions more than two miles, hence the efforts to extend his flanks with the object of surrounding them fails.
>
> The Indians select mountains for their fighting ground and positions almost impregnable. . . . The Indians are thoroughly armed and as an evidence they are abundantly supplied with ammunition, their fire in action is incessant, and nearly all the horses and mules they abandon on the march are shot.

Victorio was like a phantom to the soldiers—sometimes close but always just out of reach. Then he fled to Mexico, outside the jurisdiction of the U.S. Army, but after Victorio slaughtered 26 Mexicans the Mexican Army chased him back over the U.S. border.

Victorio then slashed his way through New Mexico, staying one step ahead of the Buffalo Soldiers. The Apache Wolf's ability to outwit and outfight his pursuers brought him new followers, including warriors from the Mescalero reservation. Colonel Hatch, suspecting that the Mescaleros were giving Victorio food and weapons, readied his troops to hunt down and surround the elusive Indian. In the meantime, Hatch said, he would visit the Mescalero reservation.

His plan was foiled by a plumbing breakdown. When a broken water pump forced the Buffalo Soldiers to lose a day of travel, Victorio and his men surrounded and attacked the regiment. Eight men were wounded, and 25 horses and mules were killed. The Indians lost one man, and Victorio vanished once more.

However, the constant pursuit enraged Victorio,

*Native Americans believed the Ghost Dance, like this Arapaho dance pictured here, would resurrect the spirits of ancestors killed in battle, cause new soil to blanket the earth and trap the white settlers below, and bring the buffalo back to the plains.*

and his attacks became more and more vicious. Word spread that he had started mutilating the bodies of the people he killed, raising the level of fear among settlers in the region. In May 1880, George Jordan and 25 other Buffalo Soldiers from the 9th Cavalry had just completed another grueling day of scouting mountain trails when they received word that Chief Victorio was headed for the nearby town of Tularosa, New Mexico. The Buffalo Soldiers postponed their much-needed rest, riding through the night to reach Tularosa. As they neared the town, the citizens ran from their houses, waving towels and handkerchiefs for joy at the prospect of being saved from Victorio.

The townspeople pleaded with the soldiers to find and attack Victorio. Jordan explained that their orders were to protect the people in the town, not to hunt down Victorio, and the soldiers built a stockade and small fort in anticipation of the Apache Wolf's arrival. Victorio and his men struck at dusk. Many times the Indians tried to get past the stockade, but the soldiers kept them away, saving many townspeople's lives. George Jordan was awarded the Congressional Medal of Honor for his leadership.

In desperation, Victorio led his men to Texas. The 10th Cavalry prepared for his arrival, stationing soldiers at the water holes and mountain passes where the renegade chief was likely to go. In August 1880, the Apaches headed for the springs at Rattlesnake Canyon, desperate for water. Knowing that Victorio would have to stop there, Grierson had already positioned his men at the springs for an ambush. Sensing that something was wrong, the chief halted and then moved forward again. The Buffalo Soldiers made their move. The battle lasted all day. Victorio retreated, and the ensuing five-day chase ended only after the soldiers' horses gave out.

A few days later, the 10th Cavalry and the Apaches met again, and the soldiers killed and wounded more than 30 Indians and chased the rest into Mexico. Vic-

torio never came back to the United States. In October 1880, the Apache Wolf and most of his men were
surrounded and killed by the Mexican Army in the
hills near Chihuahua. Although the Mexicans had
stopped Victorio's rampage, it was the hard work of
the Buffalo Soldiers that brought him closer to his
end. In *The Buffalo Soldiers*, Leckie noted:

> Mexican troops had killed Victorio and most of his war-
> riors and brought an end to the war. In a very real sense,
> however, they had only delivered the *coup de grace*. The
> real victors were the Buffalo Soldiers of the Ninth and
> Tenth Cavalry. They had pursued and fought the great
> chief over thousands of blood-spattered miles in an un-
> relenting contest of courage, skill, endurance and attrition.
>   Twice Hatch had forced Victorio into Mexico and
> with a modicum of cooperation from Mexican troops
> could have ended the struggle. When Victorio turned
> into Texas, he marched into the jaws of disaster. Grier-
> son's campaign was a model of its kind, a masterpiece
> of guerilla warfare. Not an Indian penetrated the set-
> tlements, the Apaches were outfought and outmarched,
> denied access to food and water, and driven . . . into
> Mexico. Beaten, dispirited and sapped of the will to
> fight, Victorio was an easy target for the final thrust.

However, the U.S. government gave little credit
to the Buffalo Soldiers for their role in destroying Victorio. In fact, Hatch and Grierson were ridiculed and
criticized, and the black soldiers were caricatured as
dim-witted, clumsy buffoons who could not think or
act for themselves. Two officers did praise the troopers, though. At the end of the long campaign against
Victorio, General Pope said that "Everything the men
could do they did [although] their services in the field
were marked by unusual hardships and difficulties.
Their duties were performed with zeal and intelligence
and they are worthy of all consideration." And General Ord, a man known for his dislike of black soldiers, wrote, "They are entitled to more than com-
mendation. . . . In this connection I beg to invite
attention to the long and severe service of the Tenth

Cavalry, in the field and at remote frontier stations, in this department."

Grierson had another reason to be proud of his men. As Leckie describes in *The Buffalo Soldiers:*

> They had marched, fought and scouted in the best traditions of the service. Equally their behavior in camp and station left little to be desired. Desertions in 1880, despite the most rigorous campaign in the regiment's history, reached an all-time low of five—the best record by far of any regiment in the country. Other violations of the military code were few in number: four cases of theft, one "neglect of duty," one assault and battery, "three Absent Without Leave," one "sleeping on post," one "leaving post as sentinel," one "selling of clothing," and two lesser offenses. By contrast the [white] 8th Cavalry, stationed adjacent to the 10th, had exactly twice this number of offenses."

Praise aside, the Buffalo Soldiers had no time for rest. By 1885, most of the Native American tribes had been herded onto reservations. The West was full of new towns, migrating easterners, and a wild frontier spirit. While the 10th Cavalry was in the southwest, engaged in the final stages of the Apache War, the 9th Cavalry was called to the Northern Plains, home of the Sioux Indians.

The Sioux, limited to reservations in North and South Dakota, were poor and hungry. Although life on the Sioux reservations seemed peaceful to outsiders, the Native Americans were restless because of their poverty and poor living conditions. The Sioux yearned for the freedom they had once enjoyed, and found hope in the Ghost Dance religion, which convinced them that new soil would blanket the earth, trapping the white people below. They believed that the ghost of each Indian killed in battle was coming back and that the buffalo would return to the plains. Sioux leaders encouraged everyone to dance so that this renewal of their old way of life would occur.

Throughout the reservations, the Sioux people

danced and danced while eagerly awaiting the promised changes. Their dances frightened the whites, who mistakenly assumed that the movements meant the Indians were about to go to war. A government official reported, "Indians are dancing in the snow and are wild and crazy. . . . We need protection and we need it now."

With hopes of calming tensions and avoiding bloodshed, half of the U.S. Army, including several companies of Buffalo Soldiers, moved onto or near the reservations. The appearance of so many troops had the opposite effect, however. Unrest grew among the Sioux, who feared they were about to be slaughtered. The army blamed Chief Sitting Bull, leader of the Sioux, for much of the unrest and for inciting his people to dance. Sitting Bull was the oldest and most respected of the Sioux chiefs, a strong and confident leader who once declared, "If the Great Spirit has cho-

*Sioux Chief Sitting Bull urged his poor and hungry tribe to perform the Ghost Dance to bring back the Native American way of life. However, the dances worried neighboring settlers, and U.S. troops were sent to the Sioux reservation. In the fighting that followed, Sitting Bull was killed.*

*Two weeks after Sitting Bull was killed, 350 Sioux camped at Wounded Knee Creek were attacked by a U.S. cavalry unit. Over 150 were killed immediately, and nearly as many died later of their wounds or from exposure to the cold. The massacre at Wounded Knee in 1890 marked the end of Native American resistance to settlement of the American West.*

sen anyone to be the chief of this country, it is myself."

General Nelson A. Miles believed he could end the dances and unrest, as well as the threat felt by nearby settlers, by arresting Sitting Bull. On his orders, the army arrested the Sioux chief on December 15, 1890. His followers erupted in anger and moved in to protect their leader. In the chaos that followed, Sitting Bull was killed. Hundreds of Sioux, fearful that they would be killed too, ran from the reservation to hide in the rocky, rough area known as the Badlands.

The 9th Cavalry was sent out after those who had fled. The weather at the time was, in one soldier's words, "so cold the spit froze when it left your mouth." Because tents would attract attention, the Buffalo Soldiers were forced to sleep under the stars in the frigid night air.

The 7th Cavalry, made up of white troops, found 350 Sioux camped at Wounded Knee Creek. The Indians slept in their tepees and in army tents. On December 29, 1890, the soldiers ordered the Sioux men to surrender their guns. The Sioux weapons were collected, but the soldiers were suspicious and searched the tents for hidden weapons. A young Sioux named Black Coyote held a fancy new rifle over his head, refusing to give it up. The soldiers fought him for the gun, a shot rang out, and the soldiers panicked and began shooting. One survivor, Louise Weasel Bear, recalled, "We tried to run, but they shot us like buffalo." When the bullets stopped flying, more than 300 men, women and children of the Sioux nation lay dead or dying on the frosty ground of Wounded Knee.

Word of the massacre quickly reached other nearby Sioux, who rushed to avenge the deaths of their kinsmen. The commander of the 7th Cavalry sent an urgent message asking the Buffalo Soldiers, who were still out on patrol, for reinforcements. The Buffalo Soldiers responded as quickly as they could, riding all night to reach their fellow soldiers. They arrived to find the 7th pinned down by Sioux warriors. The Buffalo Soldiers split into two groups and drove off the Sioux warriors by pursuing them from two directions.

"For all practical purposes," Clinton Cox writes, "the fighting on the Pine Ridge Reservation was over, and the Native American struggle to hold on to the land was also over."

The Buffalo Soldiers were among the last to leave Pine Ridge. They stayed there until March, and then returned to their forts in Kansas, Wyoming, and Utah. Before they and the others departed, however, General Miles held a grand review of the regiments at Pine Ridge. When the Buffalo Soldiers appeared, the general raised his white-gloved hand in salute. It was a moment to be savored, for the respect and admiration the Buffalo Soldiers had earned on the battlefield would not always follow them home.

# 4

## The Fight for Equality

FOR THE BUFFALO Soldiers, life on the battlefield often was more tolerable than life at home in post–Civil War America. Although slavery had been outlawed and African-American men given the right to vote, segregation, prejudice, and unequal treatment endured. Black people could be arrested simply for using the wrong rest rooms, hotels, and businesses. They were prohibited from owning guns and could not leave their houses at night. A black man or woman who married a white person risked imprisonment. In Mississippi, the law prevented blacks from owning farmland. Most southerners agreed with South Carolina Governor B. F. Perry, who said that his was "a white man's government, intended for white men only."

While segregation did not officially exist in the northern states, blacks did not receive equal treatment there either. African Americans were not able to get good jobs or housing. Blacks and whites rarely mixed in social or business circles; for the most part, they lived, worshiped, and attended schools among people of their own race.

Despite their long record of service to the nation, and despite the sacrifices they had made, the Buffalo Soldiers suffered the same fate as other blacks when

*Although slavery was abolished after the Civil War, African Americans were not treated equally and had to overcome poverty and prejudice wherever they lived.*

it came to life back home. As Clinton Cox writes:

> While black soldiers were fighting Native Americans in the West, black men, women, and children were being lynched, segregated, and disenfranchised in the East. The government the soldiers fought for in the Great Plains rarely lifted a finger to help the soldiers at home and often joined in their oppression.

The Buffalo Soldiers learned not to expect justice in their interactions with white civilians. For example, in 1870 a jury set free a white settler accused of killing Private Boston Henry of the 9th Cavalry in cold blood and then killing two other black soldiers in his effort to elude the law. Incidents like this occurred with disturbing frequency.

In 1881, Private William Watkins, 10th Cavalry, was singing and dancing at a saloon in San Angelo, Texas. When Watkins took a break, a white rancher named Tom McCarthy ordered him to keep singing. Watkins politely explained that he was too tired to continue. McCarthy shot him in the head.

The sheriff of San Angelo didn't see any reason to hold McCarthy in jail for something as minor as the murder of a black man and set him free until his trial. Some of the Buffalo Soldiers responded to this by distributing a notice in San Angelo that read: "We, the soldiers of the U.S. Army do hereby warn for the first and last time all citizens, cowboys, etc., of San Angelo and vicinity to recognize our right of way as just and peaceable men." An Austin, Texas, jury found McCarthy innocent of any crime. Anger rippled through the ranks of the Buffalo Soldiers, but there was little they could do. Mindful of the potential for further conflict, Grierson restricted his soldiers to Fort Concho for the entire summer.

Although African Americans had greater opportunities in the army than in civilian life, there was racial discrimination. Many of those who sought advancement were turned away or harassed. Racial bias

at the U.S. Military Academy at West Point was so severe that only three of the 20 blacks admitted to the school in the 19th century graduated. One black student, Johnson C. Whittaker, had performed well in his course work. But in his third year at the academy, he was found tied to his bed, his hair cut and his ears slashed. At a court martial he was charged with injuring himself and falsely accusing others of the crime. Ultimately, he was expelled from West Point.

Lieutenant Henry O. Flipper met with more success than did Whittaker. In 1877, Flipper made history as the first black man to graduate from West Point. After graduation, Flipper went west to command troops in the 10th Cavalry. In his autobiography *My American Journey*, General Colin Powell comments

*The class of 1880, United States Military Academy at West Point, included one African American, Johnson C. Whittaker (second row, far left). However, unfair charges were drummed up against Whittaker, and he was dismissed from the academy. Because of the racial pressures and a deep-seated opposition to African-American officers, only 3 of the 20 blacks admitted to West Point in the 19th century graduated.*

*In 1877, Henry O. Flipper became the first African American to graduate from West Point. One hundred years after his graduation, a bust of Flipper was unveiled in the academy's library.*

on Flipper's enormous accomplishment:

> Imagine a child born into slavery, yet possessing the grit to get himself admitted to the U.S. Military Academy in 1873, just ten years after Emancipation. Every black cadet before Flipper had been shunned, reviled, and ultimately hounded from West Point. Flipper took it all for four years without breaking and graduated in 1877.

Flipper, whose father had been a Georgia slave, was strong-willed, intelligent and innovative. The young lieutenant solved a problem with stagnant water, a breeding ground for disease-laden mosquitoes, by inventing a drainage system, and during the hunt for Chief Victorio, Flipper rode day and night to tell his commanding officer the warring chief's location.

After Victorio's capture, Lieutenant Flipper was transferred to Fort Davis, Texas. His commanding officer, Colonel William Shafter, and other whites at Fort Davis resented the handsome, educated black soldier. They didn't like the fact that he was an officer. They were further angered by the stories of Flipper's friendship with a young white woman named Molly Dwyer.

While at Fort Davis, Lieutenant Flipper was given the responsibility of running the post store, a job that included handling large sums of money. Flipper went out of his way to prove that he was up to the task. "Never did a man walk the path of uprightness straighter than I did," he wrote. He could never rest, knowing that the other officers were always watching, waiting for him to make a mistake. Even the smallest error, he knew, would give the white officers the excuse they needed to declare that blacks should not hold officer rank.

In July 1881, Flipper discovered that his store's funds were short. He reasoned that the best thing to do was to repay them, bit by bit, with his own money rather than inform Shafter, who would certainly blame him. That is exactly what happened when Shafter discovered that money was missing. Shafter accused Flipper of stealing the money and had him arrested, even though officers accused of nonviolent crimes were usually confined to quarters. A court martial found Flipper innocent of stealing the $3,791.77 but convicted him of conduct unbecoming an officer. Flipper maintained that he had been set up by Shafter and two other white officers. Nevertheless, the army gave Flipper a dishonorable discharge, his military career ruined at the age of 25.

Although many of the officers approved of the treatment Flipper received, others were outraged. Captain Merritt Barber of the 16th Infantry Regiment, who voluntarily defended Flipper during his court martial, denounced the verdict. "The department commander, the secretary of war, and the president of the United States [Chester A. Arthur], in dismissing the army's only black officer, tacitly voiced their opinion that no Negro was fit to bear the responsibility and prestige attached to the uniform of an officer of the United States Army," Barber argued.

Despite his disgrace, Flipper had several successful careers outside of the army—as an author, mining engineer, surveyor, newspaper editor, and aide to a U.S. senator. He was instrumental in developing the Alaskan railway system. He failed, however, in nine attempts to have Congress wipe the dishonorable discharge from his record. Henry Flipper died in 1940, unable to right his name.

Thanks to the efforts of Ray MacColl, a white Georgia schoolteacher, Henry Flipper's record was cleared eventually. In 1970, MacColl took a black history class and became fascinated with Flipper's story. He joined forces with Irsle King, Flipper's niece, and they appealed to the army to review Flipper's record. An investigation revealed that Flipper had been framed by the white officers just as he had claimed, and in 1976, nearly forty years after his death, Henry Flipper was given his long-overdue honorable discharge. On the 100th anniversary of Flipper's graduation from West Point, a bust of him was unveiled, and it is now exhibited in the Cadet Library.

The two other black men who graduated from West Point in the nineteenth century were John Alexander, who graduated in 1887, and Charles Young, who graduated in 1889. Alexander served as an officer with the 9th Cavalry for seven years and died in 1894 while on active duty. A military post in Virginia was named Camp Alexander in his honor.

Young was assigned to the 10th Cavalry Regiment and his long career included participation in the Spanish-American War, service in the Philippines, and command of the 10th Cavalry under General John J. Pershing in Mexico during the hunt for Mexican outlaw Pancho Villa. At the beginning of World War I, Colonel Young was removed from active duty because doctors said he had high blood pressure. Although he rode 500 miles on horseback in 16 days to prove his fitness, the decision stood. In 1918, he was restored to active duty, and he was sent to Liberia two years later to help reorganize that African country's army. He died in 1922 in Nigeria and was buried with full honors at Arlington National Cemetery.

It would be nearly 50 years after Young's graduation from West Point before another black man would graduate from the U.S. Military Academy.

The injustices of the 19th century symbolize the tragic results of racial hatred and discrimination. Blacks struggled for equality inside the military and out. Progress was slow, and setbacks were frequent. Like most African Americans, the Buffalo Soldiers loved their country despite its flaws and served it without hesitation. As General Powell wrote:

> A certain ambivalence has always existed among African Americans about military service. Why should we fight for a country that, for so long, did not fight for us, that in fact denied us our fundamental rights? . . .
>
> Why have blacks, nevertheless, always answered the nation's call? They have done so to exercise their rights as citizens in the one area where it was permitted. They did it because they believed that if they demonstrated equal courage and equal sacrifice in fighting and dying for their country, then equality of opportunity surely must follow.

*Charles Young had a distinguished military career after his graduation from West Point in 1889, becoming the first African American to achieve the rank of colonel. He led troops in the famous charge up San Juan Hill during the Spanish-American War, and he later was appointed military attaché to the American delegation in Liberia, Africa.*

# 5

On the Frontier

THE FRONTIER WAS not an easy place to live, for black soldiers or white. Most of the forts were ragged collections of shacks. Soldiers slept on rough, bug-infested bunks, packed into barracks unfit for human habitation. They had no indoor bathtubs or showers. Many men fell ill from the filth. Colds and diarrhea were common. More soldiers were killed by tuberculosis on the frontier than died in the Indian Wars.

On a typical day, the Buffalo Soldiers rose before daybreak to feed their horses. After an early breakfast, they practiced drills, stood guard, and took care of their horses. They ate dinner around noon. Their food, like their horses and equipment, was inferior to that given to the white troops. According to the post surgeon at Fort Concho, New Mexico, the black soldiers were fed the worst meat, foul canned peas, and sour bread. "They had none of the staples common at other posts," William Leckie writes. "The butter was made of suet [animal fat] and there was only enough flour for the officers." Most of their horses came from white cavalry regiments after they had been ruined or rejected, a situation that prompted frequent complaints from Colonel Grierson.

*The 9th Cavalry Band before a performance in Santa Fe, New Mexico, circa 1880.*

Some Buffalo Soldiers marched in full uniforms Sunday through Friday nights while the post band played and the American flag was lowered for the night. Others used evenings to learn to read and write. The black cavalrymen often dressed casually for their work on the trail, riding in blue flannel shirts or gray undershirts, often with American or Mexican army hats. After weeks on the trail, most of the Buffalo Soldiers' pants were worn or torn. But they worked hard, fought proudly, and rarely complained to anyone. A visiting newspaper reporter described the black soldiers as "active, intelligent and resolute men [who] appear to me to be rather superior to the average white men recruited in time of peace. Their officers explain this by saying that the best colored young men can be recruited in time of peace."

The western territory was a constant challenge to the Buffalo Soldiers. Temperatures ranged from very hot to extremely cold, and wild animals were a constant threat. The soldiers often had to patrol unknown, unmapped territory, cross large deserts, and navigate treacherous mountain passes. While the locals sometimes provided assistance, they were often more of a hindrance than a help.

During the summer of 1877, 40 soldiers from the 10th Cavalry came to an unfamiliar part of the Texas plains. Their guide, a Mexican, assured them that he knew the area well. The sun beat down and the soldiers rationed each sip of water in their canteens. Without water, they would surely die in a day or two. The guide urged them on, swearing that water was near. Eventually, he deserted the soldiers, probably afraid to admit that he was lost.

Heat and thirst caused several soldiers to faint. Some fell behind. One of the commanding officers, Lieutenant Charles Cooper, reported that "their tongues and throats were swollen, and they were unable even to swallow their saliva—in fact, they had no saliva to swallow." Some of the horses died of exhaustion and thirst. Cooper told the men to slit the horses' throats and drink their blood. "The fourth day without water was dreadful," Cooper said, describing "men gasping in death . . . horses falling dead to the right and left; the crazed survivors . . . fighting his neighbor for the blood of horses."

Relief came when the soldiers found Double Lakes, where they quenched their thirst, refilled their canteens, and took water to the men who had fallen behind. Thirty-six of the men survived the ordeal; four died from thirst and desert heat.

Life in frontier towns was often just as challenging as life on the open frontier, although in different ways. The 9th Cavalry was called on to bring order to towns such as Lincoln, New Mexico, where Billy the Kid, a gunman who claimed he had killed 21 people by the time he was 19 years old, and other outlaws ran wild.

Gunfights were so common in Lincoln that it was unsafe for citizens to walk the streets. In early 1878, the governor of New Mexico requested assistance from the U.S. Army. Captain George Purington took 25 members of the 9th Cavalry to Lincoln. Uncertain how to proceed, Purington advised the gunmen to take their bloody battles to the mountains, and the Buffalo Soldiers returned to Fort Concho.

By spring, the fighting in Lincoln was so bad that the sheriff and two deputies were gunned down in the street. In July, nearly a hundred outlaws stormed Lincoln, took cover in stores and houses, and began a four-day spree of nonstop shooting. Many outlaws were hurt or killed. Only when a businessman was killed and his house burned to the ground did the gunfire briefly halt. The situation in Lincoln became so dangerous that the president of the United States ordered the army to halt the marauding.

The 9th Cavalry helped make the streets of Lincoln a great deal safer for residents of the town. In return for their trouble, members of the 9th were

*The Seminole Negro Indian Scouts were descended from runaway slaves who married into Seminole Indian bands in Florida before the Civil War. The scouts were recruited by the U.S. Army to help fight the Plains Indians.*

routinely insulted by the white citizens of Lincoln. Racial tensions sometimes flared dangerously. In 1878 white rioters assaulted a black sergeant. In response, soldiers from the 10th Cavalry went looking for the whites and had a shootout with them. When a bullet wounded one of the black troopers, his comrades, according to Katz in *The Black West*, "rode out of Fort Concho, armed and led by their sergeant, entered the saloon hangout of the whites, and after a fast drink at the bar, spun and fired into the crowd, killing all."

The Buffalo Soldiers were not the only black military men on the frontier. The Seminole Negro Indian Scouts were descended from runaway slaves who left the south for Florida before the Civil War. The ex-slaves lived with and married into the Seminole Indian bands that made their homes in Florida. Eventually, President Andrew Jackson's Indian removal policy forced the black Indians to venture west. When whites tried to return the black Indians and their children to slavery, they moved to Mexico, where they became known for their superior fighting and tracking abilities. In 1870, when the U.S. Army needed scouts to help fight the Plains Indians, it recruited the black Indians with promises of land and food.

At first, the Seminole Negro Indian Scouts were led by one of their own, Chief John Kibbett. In 1872, a white former Civil War officer named Lt. John Bullis took over. He praised the scouts in every area except military appearance because they wore traditional Indian dress with feathered war bonnets rather than standard-issue military uniforms.

Bullis led the men for nine years. During that time they were in both cavalry and infantry regiments and worked with black and white soldiers. The company never lost a man in battle or had one seriously injured in 12 major engagements.

Joseph Phillips, a member of the Scouts, said, "The Scouts thought a lot of Bullis. . . . That fella suffer just like we-all did out in de woods. He was a good man. He was a Injun fighter. He was tuff. . . . He didn't stand and say, 'Go yonder'; he would say 'Come on boys, let's go get 'em.'"

Bullis' closeness with his men saved his life on more than one occasion. In April 1875, Bullis and three scouts ran into some Comanche Indians as they tried to cross the Pecos River. When Bullis lost his horse, the Comanches went after the lieutenant. Unwilling to leave Bullis unprotected, the three scouts rode directly at the attacking Indians, firing their guns. Bullis jumped onto a horse ridden by one of the scouts, and they returned to camp uninjured. Bullis arranged for all three scouts to receive the Congressional Medal of Honor.

The government was less forthcoming on its earlier promises, however. The land and food promised the Seminole Negro Indian Scouts never materialized.

*Lieutenant John Bullis commanded the Seminole Negro Indian Scouts for nine years and was highly respected by his men. Under Bullis, the Scouts never lost a man in battle.*

Hunger forced the men and their families to scavenge and steal food, and scout leaders submitted several petitions for better treatment. Despite strong support from Lieutenant Bullis and other officers, the U.S. government failed to deliver on its promises.

By 1881, the scouts were no longer part of the U.S. Army, victims of prejudice and racial hostility. As Katz states in *The Black West*, "The unit . . . could survive the Texas desert and savage warfare, but not the traditional racism of the federal government or its citizens."

Unlike their brethren in the Seminole Negro Indian Scouts, the Buffalo Soldiers continued to serve their country despite the often thankless work and a constant barrage of abuse. In the 1880s they faced a new and frustrating assignment: keeping settlers known as "Boomers" from taking over part of the Oklahoma Indian Territory. This area was known as the Unassigned Lands because it was not yet designated for a specific tribe.

The 9th Cavalry was told to move the Boomers out, since their presence on the lands was against the law. The Boomers, so named because of their plan to create an economic boom in the southwest from which they would profit, claimed the Indian Territory as their own, building homes and schools and farming the land.

The U.S. government could either give the Oklahoma land to the Indian tribes, who had been promised the territory in earlier treaties, or open it to

*In the 1880s, groups of settlers attempted to move into the Oklahoma Territory, which had been designated for Native Americans. The settlers were known as "Boomers" for their attempts to create a land boom in the southwest. The Buffalo Soldiers were called to peacefully escort Boomers out of the Oklahoma Territory many times.*

settlers and railroads, representing money and political power. While trying to make a decision, the government sent armed soldiers to keep trespassers off the land. The Buffalo Soldiers at Fort Sill, Fort Reno, and Fort Supply were part of this assignment.

At the center of the fragmented Boomer movement was a man named David L. Payne. Hundreds of Boomers united under Payne's leadership. In 1880 he challenged the government's power to keep his followers from taking the land they claimed as their own. Payne's first settlement was near what is now Oklahoma City. Within a year, he had taken over more land. The Boomers went into—and were removed from—that area four times in 1882 alone. They were fined amounts up to $100,000, but had no money and made no attempt to pay. By 1882, Payne had attracted 900 followers. All were armed, and all vowed to resist and defy the federal government until the land was theirs.

Members of the 9th Cavalry sympathized with the Boomers' ambitions, if not their tactics, and treated them accordingly. Sometimes they even shared their rations with the hungry settlers. More than once, the black cavalrymen managed to lead the Boomers out of their settlements without incident or bloodshed. Other times, though, they were forced to take drastic action. On one occasion, when a group of Boomers refused to obey orders to vacate a piece of land, the Buffalo Soldiers tied their hands and feet and carted them off the land in wagons.

By the spring of 1884, patience on both sides had worn thin and the generally cordial relations between the army and the Boomers had come to an end. A telling event occurred in May 1884, when a white lieutenant, in a sudden fit of anger, ordered the Buffalo Soldiers to fire on a group of Boomers who had crossed forbidden lines and established camp illegally. The black soldiers refused to shoot the settlers. Within moments, the lieutenant regained his composure. At the

same time, the Boomers realized how close they had come to dying and peacefully submitted to arrest. The Buffalo Soldiers were neither reprimanded nor punished for disobeying their commanding officer, for all realized that only the discipline and composure of the black soldiers had prevented a tragedy from taking place.

The final stand under David Payne took place in June 1884, when 1,500 Boomers were discovered living in Rock Falls. Colonel Hatch ordered the settlers to move on or be driven out by the army. Most of the Boomers heeded the Colonel's words, but 250 refused to leave. The Buffalo Soldiers had to move them out by force. Then, to make sure the Boomers didn't re-

*In 1893, President Benjamin Harrison opened the Oklahoma Territory to all, setting off the Oklahoma Land Rush. On March 23, 1893, over 50,000 people, 20 percent of them African American, started at the state border and raced to claim a piece of the territory.*

turn, the soldiers burned their barns and houses to the ground.

When Payne died in November of that year, his followers carried on the struggle for a time. In December, the 9th Cavalry discovered 300 Boomers living near Stillwater Creek. The settlers announced that they would not leave without a fight. Wanting to avoid violence and bloodshed, Colonel Hatch devised a strategy for peaceful evacuation. The soldiers were placed outside the settlement to prevent wagons with food from reaching the Boomers. After a few days without food, the Boomers left without incident.

Although the Army eventually managed to get the illegal settlement problem under control, the effort proved pointless when, on March 23, 1893, President Benjamin Harrison declared the Unassigned Lands fair game to settlers. The Buffalo Soldiers were called to maintain order, and on that day the Oklahoma Land Rush began, with more than 50,000 people —some 10,000 of them black—waiting at the state border for the chance to claim a piece of the newly available territory.

In less than a week, shacks, tents, and storefronts bloomed in what had been known as the Wild West. The frontier, according to the director of the U.S. Bureau of the Census in Washington, D.C., had officially ceased to exist.

In 1888, Colonel Grierson turned the command of the 10th Cavalry over to a young officer. On that day Grierson declared that "the officers and enlisted men have cheerfully endured many hardships and privations, and in the midst of great dangers steadfastly maintained a most gallant and zealous devotion to duty, and they may well be proud of the record made." Colonel Hatch died at Fort Robinson, Nebraska, in April 1889, after 23 years of leading the 9th Cavalry regiment.

Within a few years, many of the original Buffalo Soldiers would die or retire. Some, like Henry Mc-

Clain, would take up farming. Others, like George Jordan, would become leaders in their communities. Several would take advantage of their skill with horses to hire on at ranches throughout the West. However, they would not achieve what might have been their greatest dream, which was to build a country that respected them and their people.

The 1880s marked the end of an era for the brave, devoted men known as the Buffalo Soldiers. Those who would carry on their tradition would fight many of their next battles on foreign soil.

# 6

## To Cuba

THE NEXT CHAPTER of the Buffalo Soldiers' story was written in Cuba, a tropical island 90 miles off the coast of Florida. Cuba had come under Spanish control in 1511, and over the years Spanish traders had earned handsome profits from Cuba's sugar, tobacco, and other raw materials. Cuba also had become a matter of national pride for Spain, which saw most of its other colonies slip away during the 19th century. The Cubans were not as impressed with Spain as Spain was with Cuba, however. The Cuban people rebelled twice against Spanish rule, first in 1868 and again in 1895. Spain brutally crushed both uprisings with little difficulty.

Americans took an interest in the struggle occurring so close to their shores. They sympathized with the Cuban independence movements, recalling their own struggle for freedom from British colonial rule. Newspapers reported stories of the Cuban peoples' suffering and encouraged Americans to support them. The island's fight for freedom was described by one newspaper as "blood on the doorstep" of America. The narrow distance separating Spanish troops and ships

*Members of the 9th Cavalry, carrying their gear, prepare to board a train for Florida. From there, the troops sailed to Cuba on transport ships under hot, unsanitary conditions.*

63

*The explosion of the battleship U.S.S. Maine in Havana harbor killed 260 U.S. sailors and fueled anti-Spanish sentiment, leading to the Spanish-American War in 1898.*

from the United States worried Americans; Spain had numerous times interfered in trade between Cuba and America, fueling growing resentment toward the continued European presence in the Western Hemisphere.

In a gesture of friendship toward the Cuban people and in a show of force aimed at Spain, the U.S. government sent a battleship, the *U.S.S. Maine,* to Cuba's Havana Harbor. On the evening of February 15, 1898, the *Maine* exploded and sank, killing 260 crew members. The cause of the blast was never discovered, but many Americans blamed the Spanish. The rallying cry for Americans became "Remember the *Maine!*"

By April 1898, the president and Congress were convinced that Spain would not grant Cuba its independence. Nevertheless, the United States demanded that Cuba be set free and almost immediately began a blockade of Cuban ports. Spain responded by declaring war on the United States on April 23. The Spanish-American War had begun.

Twenty-eight thousand American servicemen, including the U.S. Army's four African-American regiments, fought in the Spanish-American War. The Spanish-American War marked two firsts for blacks in American history: it was the first time black soldiers fought for their country on foreign soil and the first time blacks served under the command of black officers in battle.

The Buffalo Soldiers left the Northern Plains and took a train to Tampa, Florida, where the troops would depart for Cuba. Once again, the government treated its black soldiers with less respect than its white soldiers. The government did not provide the black troops with the lighter uniforms they needed for the tropical climate, so they took the only uniforms they owned —hot, heavy wool guaranteed to keep them in a state of discomfort.

The ride to Florida also was filled with reminders of the racist sentiments still held by many Americans. In Minnesota, rail stations were bedecked with flags and flowers to honor the black troops. Such tributes lessened as they neared the south and in one southern city, a barber put up a sign demanding that blacks stay away from his shop. Sergeant Frank W. Pullen reported that "there was no enthusiasm nor Stars and Stripes in Georgia."

Even before the departure for Cuba, racism surfaced again. On the *U.S.S. Concho*, Government Transport 14, the 25th regiment was segregated from the white 14th Infantry. The blacks were forced to stay on the lower deck where, as Pullen described:

> There was no light, except the small portholes when the gangplank was closed. So dark was it that candles were burned all day. There was no air except what came down the canvas air-shafts when they were turned to the breeze. The heat of the place was almost unendurable. Still our Brigade Commander issued orders that no one would be allowed to sleep on the main deck. That order was the only one to my knowledge that was not obeyed by the colored soldiers.

Transport 14 waited at the dock in Tampa for a

*Teddy Roosevelt and the Rough Riders gained fame for their charge up San Juan Hill during the Spanish-American War. What has never been as well known is the Buffalo Soldiers' important role in that battle.*

week before setting sail for Cuba. While white troops moved around freely, Pullen said, blacks "were not allowed to go ashore, unless an officer would take a whole company off to bathe and exercise." The black soldiers also received orders that they should make coffee for whites, and that the two races should not mix, even though these same men had served peacefully together in Montana.

The ships carrying American soldiers reached Cuba on June 22. Among them were four black regiments: the 9th and 10th Cavalries and the 24th and 25th Infantry units. Soldiers climbed through the portholes, dropping 15 feet to steam-powered boats that took them to shore. The jump was made harder by the gear each soldier had to carry: tent, blanket roll, rifle, ammunition, poncho, and three days' worth of food. The following day, the cavalry regiments headed inland, joining a group headed for Las Guasimas in the Cuban hills. The difficult trek through thick jungle forced the men to walk slowly, often in single file.

One of the 10th Cavalry's first acts at Las Guasimas was to help save the Rough Riders, a celebrated volunteer regiment consisting of former Confederate soldiers, Indian fighters, New York City athletes, shopkeepers, and others. The most famous member of the regiment was its second-in-command, Lieutenant Colonel Theodore Roosevelt. Roosevelt had resigned from his position as undersecretary of the navy on the day the United States entered the war against Spain. Although his regiment was not a regular army unit and was not scheduled to take part in the war, Roosevelt wanted to fight. He managed to get his regiment to Cuba, although much of their equipment and many of their pack animals were lost during the landing. With few guns and animals, the Rough Riders had no chance against the Spanish soldiers who fired at them as they struggled through the dense Cuban bush.

The Buffalo Soldiers called upon their Indian War strategies to help their fellow Americans. Creeping past the Rough Riders on the right and the left, the black troopers beat back the Spaniards. According to a white officer, "the Rough Riders would have been exterminated" without the assistance and skill of the Buffalo Soldiers. Individual acts also brought accolades. For example, Private Augustus Wally of the 9th Cavalry earned a Congressional Medal of Honor for running through a hail of bullets to carry a wounded officer to safety.

Shortly after the encounter at Las Guasimas, the Buffalo Soldiers helped to bring about two other important victories. On July 1, American forces were ordered to capture Spanish hilltop fortifications on Kettle Hill and San Juan Hill, both located on the outskirts

*African-American fighting units deserved much of the credit for the American capture of San Juan Hill. However, their courageous actions were ignored after the battle.*

of the city of Santiago de Cuba. The attacking American forces charged the two hills without benefit of artillery fire, which would have weakened their Spanish foes. Soldiers literally had to crawl through the jungle while dodging Spanish bullets. As the 9th Cavalry and Rough Riders moved toward Kettle Hill, the 10th Cavalry headed for San Juan Hill. At San Juan Hill, Sergeant Thomas Griffith of the 10th cleared a path for his comrades, crawling ahead and removing barbed wire that the Spanish had woven through the trees and bushes. Using tactics honed through long years on the American frontier, the Buffalo Soldiers confused the Spanish soldiers into firing aimlessly at their opponents.

The sight of a racially integrated fighting force inspired Lieutenant John J. Pershing, a white officer with the 10th Cavalry. "White regiments, black regiments, regulars and Rough Riders, representing the young manhood of the North and South, fought shoulder to shoulder, unmindful of race or color, unmindful of whether commanded by an ex-Confederate or not," Pershing said. The only thing that mattered to the soldiers, he recalled, was their "common duty as Americans."

The Americans claimed victory before the sun went down that day, with the army's black regiments deserving much of the credit. "It was glorious," Pershing said. "For the moment every thought was forgotten but victory. We officers of the Tenth Cavalry could have taken our black heroes in our arms." One white soldier declared, "The Negroes saved that fight." Another said, "The services of no four white regiments can be compared to those rendered by the four colored regiments—the Ninth and Tenth Cavalry and the Twenty-fourth and Twenty-fifth Infantry."

The white and black heroes of the Battle of San Juan Hill were saluted with a rousing version of "It's Gonna Be a Hot Time in the Old Town Tonight" by the 10th Cavalry band. Frank Knox, a Rough Rider who went on to serve as Secretary of War during World War II, said, "I joined a troop of the Tenth Cavalry and for a time fought with them shoulder to shoulder and in justice to the colored race I must say that I never saw braver men anywhere. Some of these who rushed up the hill will live in my memory forever."

However, joy over the victories on San Juan and Kettle hills was tempered by the high number of casualties. American losses in both battles totaled 1,385, with 205 dead and 1,180 wounded. The 10th Cavalry alone lost one out of five enlisted men and half of its officers in the push for San Juan Hill.

Within days of the American victories on San Juan and Kettle hills, the Spanish stronghold at Santiago de Cuba was surrounded by Cuban rebel forces. The Spanish realized that they could not escape, and they agreed to negotiate a surrender. The loss of Santiago de Cuba convinced the Spanish government that Spain could no longer hold Cuba. On August 12, 1898, representatives of the United States and Spain agreed to end hostilities. A treaty officially ending the war was signed on December 10, 1898.

With the war officially at an end, more than one hundred black soldiers were promoted to officer status. Six African Americans earned the Congressional Medal of Honor; five had served in the 10th Cavalry, and the sixth was a sailor on the *U.S.S. Iowa*. The efforts of the Buffalo Soldiers were even praised in a popular song called "Hats Off to the Boys Who Made Good." The lyrics included these lines:

> The millionaire clubmen, the "dudes" they would
>   dub them,
> They said that the coon boys would quit.
> But the hills of San Juan, they were first to come on,
> Did they fight for our flag? Are they it?

Theodore Roosevelt, whose Rough Riders had fought side by side with the Buffalo Soldiers and had been saved by them on at least one occasion, acknowledged in his farewell remarks the black soldiers' role in America's victory by saying, "They can drink out of our canteens." With segregation still a fact of American life, the comment implied that the Buffalo Soldiers were very much the equals of Roosevelt and his Rough Rider regiment.

Curiously, Roosevelt told an altogether different tale months later. He told white audiences that the African Americans were "peculiarly dependent upon their white officers" and said that in the heat of battle, some appeared cowardly, beginning "to get a little uneasy and to drift to the rear." He even claimed he had to draw his gun to keep the black men from backing off from the Spaniards.

Angered by these remarks, Sergeant Preston Holliday answered Roosevelt's charge with the statement that the "retreat" Roosevelt described was not a withdrawal but the result of a white officer of the Rough Riders ordering the men to halt. However, Sergeant Holliday's rebuttal was not widely circulated. Like Holliday, other members of the black units that had fought so bravely in the Spanish-American War were stung by Roosevelt's comments. Despite this and other insults, of which there were many, they carried themselves proudly.

Chaplain George Prioleau wrote, "These black boys, heroes of our country, were not allowed to stand at the counters of the restaurants and drink a cup of coffee. The white soldiers were welcomed and invited to sit down at the tables and eat free of cost. . . . It seems as if God has forgotten us." No matter what battles they won, whose lives they saved, or how much they achieved, in their own country among their fellow citizens the Buffalo Soldiers were rarely viewed as heroes.

At the turn of the century, life for African Americans was far from fair or equal; yet progress was taking place. The U.S. military, which only a short time earlier had barred blacks from full service, was opening its doors to black leadership. The 20th century began with four black commissioned officers (not including chaplains) in the U.S. Army: Captain Charles A. Young, Lieutenant Benjamin O. Davis Sr., Lieutenant John R. Lynch, and Lieutenant John E. Green. In 1940, Davis would go on to become the first black general in the United States. Trailblazers all, the African-American officers were instrumental in forging the path that would someday take a black man to the highest level of military leadership.

"I know I wouldn't be . . . where I am today, if thousands of African Americans had not prepared the way for me," General Colin Powell said in 1990. "And among the thousands, planted firmly like a great fort on the western desert, stand the Buffalo Soldiers— an everlasting symbol of man's ability to overcome, an everlasting symbol of human courage in the face of all obstacles and dangers."

# 7

# In the Trenches

THE BUFFALO SOLDIERS had paved the way for African Americans who wished to serve in the armed forces. Although the Buffalo Soldiers did not fight as a group in World War I, nearly 400,000 African Americans, 11 percent of the American fighting force, did take part. About 50 percent saw combat, serving in one of two divisions: the 92nd and 93rd. Many served with distinction. In the 92nd Division alone, 43 soldiers and 14 officers received medals for heroic fighting. Other black soldiers worked as stevedores (unloading cargo from ships) or as laborers.

Although the African-American contribution to the defeat of Spain had not brought much progress toward racial equality at home, many blacks hoped that their sacrifices for victory in World War I would finally accomplish that goal. W. E. B. DuBois, an influential black scholar and civil rights advocate, urged his fellow African Americans to put aside their grievances and help to win the war. DuBois and others were deeply disappointed by the results. Enthusiastic support for America's war effort had once again made little difference in the lives of average black Americans. Racial segregation and inequality continued much as it had before the war.

*A young recruit receives a blanket and mess kit at Fort Devens, Massachusetts, in 1918. About 11 percent of the U.S. fighting force in World War I was black, with nearly 50 percent serving in combat units such as the 92nd and 93rd Infantry Divisions.*

Within the military, life for blacks also remained largely unchanged. Black soldiers were still segregated from their white counterparts and, in most cases, received inferior equipment and training. At training camps in the United States, black soldiers often worked outdoors in near freezing temperatures without winter clothing. When barracks were provided for black soldiers—and sometimes they weren't—they often lacked the blankets, floors, and heaters that could be found in barracks housing white soldiers. Near Baltimore, 300 blacks were crowded into a building equal in size to one occupied by 35 white soldiers, Arthur E. Barbeau and Florette Henri report in *The Unknown Soldiers: African-American Troops in World War I*. Mess halls were sometimes so inadequate that soldiers had to carry their food to their tents. Food also was a problem. Barbeau and Henri note, "Food was bad, the meat scarce and sometimes unfit to eat."

Military authorities were also uncertain about how to deal with black officers. One difficult question for the War Department was whether blacks should be trained as commissioned officers. Although the idea was dismissed at first, because some people believed black men lacked leadership qualities, the persistence of the National Association for the Advancement of Colored People (NAACP), the Urban League, and black newspapers like *The Chicago Defender* eventually led to changes in the policy, and an all-black Officer Training School was established with 639 black officer candidates. However, a black officer could not command white officers or enlisted men.

In an effort to make use of black soldiers and officers, General John J. Pershing, commander in chief of the American Expeditionary Force, decided to attach African-American regiments to the allied French Army. For some time, the French had been asking for American regiments to replace their own decimated troops. Because Pershing was not sure how to use the black troops in the American effort, he decided to

give them to the French. Unlike the Americans, the French did not have a tradition of racial prejudice. Cultural and procedural difficulties were the biggest obstacles to integrating the American soldiers into the French Army. "Despite all the difficulties, somehow the black American infantry regiments of the 93rd Division became part of the French army and shared in the fight to make the world safe for democracy," Barbeau and Henri comment.

Among the regiments of the 93rd Division in France was the 369th Infantry. The 369th had been organized in 1916 in New York. It initially consisted of 10 companies of about 65 men each, all of whom had previous military experience. When the regiment later received permission to expand its numbers to reach wartime strength, some of its members were recruited by appeals made from street corners and theater stages.

*These are members of the 369th Infantry, dubbed the "Harlem Hell Fighters," which took part in many bloody battles in France, fighting in the Argonne Forest, Chateau-Thierry, and Belleau Wood. The 369th had the best combat record of any U.S. infantry regiment in the First World War.*

The 369th Infantry took part in several major and bloody battles, including those in the Argonne Forest, Chateau-Thierry, and Belleau Wood. Along with other regiments of the 93rd, the 369th fought in the offensive that finally shattered German resistance. The 369th earned the distinction of having the best record of any U.S. Army infantry regiment in World War I. Dubbed the "Harlem Hell Fighters," they made their mark with the French Army, sporting U.S. uniforms and French weaponry. The 369th was in the trenches for 191 days and never gave the Germans an inch.

African-American soldiers distinguished themselves in numerous battles of World War I, although their efforts did not always receive the recognition they deserved. Sergeant Henry Johnson of the 369th Infantry was the first American of any race to receive the French Croix de Guerre. A total of 34 black officers and 89 black enlisted men received the Croix de Guerre during the war. In the 92nd Division, 14 black officers and 34 black enlisted men earned the United States Army Distinguished Flying Cross (DFC), and 10 officers and 34 enlisted men of the 93rd Division received the DFC.

Not a single African-American serviceman received the Congressional Medal of Honor in the First World War. Decades later, in 1988, the Army combed the National Archives to see whether racism was the cause for this omission. The search uncovered a recommendation that one black man, Corporal Freddie Stowers from South Carolina, be given the award, but the paperwork for the recommendation had never been processed. Stowers, a squad leader, led his men through a wall of machine gun bullets, upsetting the enemy. He was wounded but kept leading his men through another trench line. He died of his injuries. Stowers' surviving sisters received Corporal Freddie Stowers' Congressional Medal of Honor from President George Bush at the White House in April 1991.

Segregation remained the rule of the day in the

United States. The 10th Cavalry was at Fort Leavenworth, where black and white soldiers lived separately. The former fighting men became cooks, mechanics, and clerks and took care of the white officers' horses.

As committed as ever to serving with excellence, the Buffalo Soldiers were disheartened by the army's failure to utilize their talents and skills fully. In the words of Sergeant Elmer E. Robinson, a member of the 10th Cavalry at that time, "We took so many of the hard knocks. We withstood the embarrassments. The contribution that we made as black soldiers made it possible for some of the people to be in the position that they are today." Eventually, soldiers of the 9th and 10th Cavalries were moved to other regiments, many of which fought in World War II.

*Although black soldiers shared in battlefield dangers, after World War I their skills were ignored by the U.S. Army. Segregation of black and white troops continued, African-American officers were taken off active duty, and soldiers were given menial tasks to perform.*

After World War I, many senior white army officers wanted to return to barring blacks from military service. Black commissioned officers were special targets, and most were taken off active duty when the war ended. The Army claimed that black officers should be let go because they performed poorly. Major General Charles C. Ballou, who had commanded the 93rd Infantry Division during World War I, supported these charges by reminding the army that white officer candidates had to be college graduates, while blacks could become officers with only high school educations. "In many cases," Ballou wrote in a letter, "these high school educations would have been a disgrace to any grammar school. For the parts of a machine requiring the finest steel, pot metal was provided."

Not all of the white officers felt that way. Major Thomas A. Roberts wrote that "what the progressive Negro desires today is the removal of discrimination against him; that this can be accomplished in a military sense I believe to be largely possible, but not if men of the two races are segregated."

The record of African-American troops in World War I demonstrates that they performed best when treated fairly, as by the French. The War Department did not heed this lesson when World War II broke out. It continued to operate under past racial policies until absolute necessity prompted change. "The demands of total mobilization for World War II—and the stirrings of militancy on the part of blacks—compelled the armed forces to accept large numbers of African Americans and assign them tasks that would help win the war," point out Barbeau and Henri.

Although racial segregation prevailed, the American military made changes in its treatment of black servicemen. For the first time, according to Barbeau and Henri, "black tank or artillery battalions supported white infantry, African-American fighter pilots escorted bombers with white crews, and for a brief time, late in the war in Europe, platoons of black soldiers served alongside whites in the same rifle companies."

The army also took small steps toward racial integration among officers early in World War II. To best utilize the existing officer training facilities, the Army integrated its 24 Officer Candidate Schools. The "90-day wonders" who survived the three-month course were commissioned as second lieutenants in one of the 24 U.S. Army branches. However, African-American officers were assigned only to black units.

Among the first to benefit from these changes was Benjamin O. Davis Sr., who became America's first black general in 1940. His son, Colonel Benjamin O. Davis Jr., led America's first squadron of black fighter pilots, the 99th Pursuit Squadron, in World War II.

Within weeks of the start of World War II in Europe, the NAACP and the Urban League joined forces to battle segregation. The sheer scope of the war effort generated new jobs, technology, and opportuni-

In 1936, Benjamin O. Davis Jr. (left) became the first African American to graduate from West Point in 50 years. He commanded the 332nd Fighter Group during World War II and became the first black general in the U.S. Air Force in 1954. His father, Benjamin O. Davis Sr. (right) had enlisted in the U.S. Army as a private in 1899 and rose through the ranks. In 1940, he was promoted to brigadier general, the first African American to earn that rank, and he served as special advisor to the commander of the European forces during the Second World War.

ties. Members of these organizations wanted to make sure that black Americans shared in the growth while they made the sacrifices that other Americans were making. To demonstrate their commitment to winning a war on two fronts, African Americans adopted the slogan "Double V," which symbolized the two-edged battle against foreign fascism and domestic racism. Several black activists joined with the NAACP and the Urban League to plan a march in Washington, D.C. The march organizers hoped to attract at least 100,000 people. They wanted to send the government a message that black America wanted equal treatment in all aspects of the national defense.

A week before the march was to occur, President Franklin D. Roosevelt issued Executive Order 8802, which set up a Committee on Fair Employment Practice "to provide the full and equitable participation of all workers in defense industries, without discrimination." This opened defense plant jobs to millions of African-American men and women, who were able to earn the same wages as whites. The order did not extend to the armed forces, however. Bowing to pressure from the NAACP, Roosevelt agreed to open several branches of the military and several occupational specialties to blacks. However, he ruled out troop integration because he thought it would be "destructive to morale and detrimental to . . . preparation for national defense."

In the tradition of the original Buffalo Soldiers, black military personnel continued to serve their country proudly despite the inequalities in treatment and opportunities. An African-American man named Dorie Miller, serving on the *U.S.S. Arizona*, manned a machine gun during the December 7, 1941, attack on Pearl Harbor, shooting down four enemy planes. He was awarded the Navy Cross.

Members of the Army Air Force Aviation Cadet program, where pilots, navigators, and bombardiers were trained, also demonstrated their resolve in the face of adversity. Some 926 black pilots earned their wings and commissions at the Tuskegee Army Air Field in Alabama. The more than 600 single-engine pilots went on to form the 332nd Fighter Group, which had four squadrons. One of those squadrons, the 99th Fighter Squadron, was led by Lieutenant Colonel Benjamin O. Davis Jr., a 1936 graduate of West Point.

In August 1943, Davis was assigned to lead the 332nd Fighter Group. Upon taking command, he was shocked to learn that Colonel William Momeyer, the group commander, was working to discredit the successes of the black pilots. In his appraisal of the 99th, Colonel Momeyer wrote:

> Based on the performance of the 99th Fighter Squadron to date it is my opinion that they are not of the fighting caliber of any squadron in this group. They have failed to display the aggressiveness and daring for combat that are necessary to a first class fighting organization. It may be expected that we will get less work and less operational time out of the 99th Fighter Squadron than any squadron in this group.

*African-American troops made many contributions to the American effort in World War II. These soldiers are taking a break after the Allies' largest offensive, the D-Day invasion of Normandy in June 1944.*

Commander Davis defended his squadron before the War Department's Committee on Special [Negro] Troop Policies. In the autobiography Davis wrote after retiring, he said of the incident, "It would have been hopeless for me to stress the hostility and racism of whites as the motive behind the letter, although that was clearly the case. Instead, I had to adopt a quiet, reasoned approach, presenting the facts about the 99th in a way that would appeal to fairness and win out over ignorance and racism."

Davis was so persuasive that the army ordered a special study of the black pilots, rating their readiness, squadron missions, friendly losses versus enemy losses, and sorties dispatched. The report opened by saying, "An examination of the record of the 99th Fighter Squadron reveals no significant general difference between this squadron and the balance of the P-40 squadrons in the Mediterranean Theatre of Operations."

Black ground, air, and sea forces also performed admirably and made significant contributions to the United States' victory in World War II. Their numbers alone were impressive. The all-black 93rd Infantry Division was the largest combat unit in the Pacific, and the 92nd Infantry—nicknamed the "Buffalo Division" in reference to the proud tradition of black soldiers in the west—was one of the larger army units in Europe. And although most of the one million African-American servicemen during the Second World War served in the Army, 165,000 blacks served in the Navy, 17,000 in the Marine Corps, 5,000 in the Coast Guard, 12,000 in Construction Battalions (Sea Bees), and 24,000 in the Merchant Marine.

While they faced some of the same challenges as the original Buffalo Soldiers, battling institutional racism and external foes, blacks in World War II had significant community support. Several black newspapers were critical of the government's racial policies in the armed services. In 1942, the U.S. Justice Department threatened to charge the newspapers with sedition, or inciting actions against lawful authority. The NAACP intervened, offering guidelines for government racial policies in hopes of preventing censorship of the black press.

In February 1948, President Harry S. Truman issued an executive order aimed at encouraging desegregation of the armed forces. The army, which had strong economic, emotional, and political ties to the Deep South, resisted in every possible way. A fully integrated American military was still years away.

Nevertheless, the legacy of the Buffalo Soldiers —their outstanding fighting, stubborn loyalty, and unshakable pride—informed and inspired blacks in the military for years to come. While America struggled with segregation and other facets of racism, blacks served their troubled country with diligence and dignity.

# 8

# Continuing Courage

**W**HEN THE KOREAN WAR began in 1950, desegregation of the Army was beginning. All but one of the four black regiments had been dissolved. The last all-black unit, the 24th Infantry, included professional soldiers from pre–World War II days, from the 9th and 10th Cavalries, the 25th Infantry, the 92nd and 93rd Divisions, and others. Upon arriving in Korea, the most experienced soldiers in the regiment were "determined that the 24th would give a good account of itself, erasing forever from Army minds the hated and humiliating belief that 'Negroes won't fight,'" explains military historian Clay Flair in *The Forgotten War: America in Korea.*

One major obstacle stood in the way. Most of the black professionals in the unit believed that many of the white officers assigned to senior positions in the regiment were unqualified to lead troops in combat. For example, the regiment's commander, Horton White, had previously served as an intelligence specialist and had never commanded troops in battle.

Nevertheless, members of the 24th Infantry under Captain Charles M. Bussey, a black World War II fighter pilot and commander of the 77th Combat Engineers Company, distinguished themselves quickly

*American soldiers celebrate the end of the Gulf War in 1991. Blacks and whites have fought side-by-side in U.S. military units since 1948, when President Harry Truman signed an order to desegregate the military.*

in the fight for Yechon, described by a war correspondent as "the first sizable American ground victory in the Korean War." Bussey received a Silver Star and a Purple Heart for his valiant efforts.

However, this victory and other actions by the 24th later were called into question in a controversy that extended well beyond the three-year war. Two months into the Korean Conflict, Major General William B. Kean asked that the army disband the 24th Infantry because it was "untrustworthy and incapable of carrying out missions expected of an infantry regiment." The controversy that swirled around the 24th continued into the 1990s. Some said that the 24th failed in combat. African-American veterans of the 24th and others counter that the unit's successes were accomplished despite racism.

The debate over the unit's combat record was stirred in 1961 with the publication of *South to the Naktong, North to the Yalu*, the U.S. Army's official history of the 24th regiment. This account of the regiment's efforts during the Korean War repeated Kean's charges of ineptitude and inferiority. The army was later asked to present a more balanced account of the black fighting men of the 24th, and in 1987, the U.S. Army Center of Military History was ordered to study the matter further. It took nearly ten years for the study to be completed.

The U.S. Army Center of Military History's study revealed that many black combat units, including the 24th Infantry, enjoyed success on the battlefield despite the obstacle of racism. Brigadier General John W. Moutcastle, chief of military history, wrote in the foreword to the report *Black Soldier, White Army*, "The account of what happened to the 24th Infantry is often disturbing and sometimes embarrassing. It offers important lessons for today's Army. . . . We must ensure that the injustices and misfortunes that befell the 24th never occur again."

The 24th Infantry was disbanded in October 1951.

In the summer of 1995, the Army reactivated the regiment's 1st Battalion at Fort Lewis near Tacoma, Washington. The new battalion is racially integrated.

By the time of the Vietnam War during the 1960s and 1970s, blacks were well represented among career soldiers and officers, and, in general, enjoyed better opportunities in the armed forces than in civilian life. However, the draft brought to the military many young men who had never served and did not intend to make the military their career. The young African-American men in this group, described by Wallace Terry in *Bloods: An Oral History of the Vietnam War by Black Veterans*, were often:

> just steps removed from marching in the Civil Rights Movement or rioting in the rebellions that swept the urban ghettos from Harlem to Watts. All were filled

*Although one all-black infantry regiment, the 24th Infantry, fought in the Korean conflict, most black soldiers served in Army units that previously had been segregated. These soldiers are members of the 2nd Infantry Division.*

*While the military was being integrated in the 1950s, segregation remained a way of life for African-American civilians. In most cases, blacks and whites had separate schools, churches, and even drinking fountains.*

with a new sense of black pride and purpose. They spoke loudest against the discrimination they encountered on the battlefield in decorations, promotion and duty assignments. They chose not to overlook the racial insults, cross-burnings and Confederate flags of their white comrades. They called for unity among black brothers on the battlefield to protest these indignities and provide mutual support.

When the Vietnam War escalated in the mid-1960s, the armed forces seemed the most thoroughly inte-

grated institution in America. At long last, the troops were completely integrated and blacks were in leadership positions. Praise came from the Pentagon for the brave black fighting men, who were dying in greater numbers than Americans of other races.

Americans were divided over the war in Vietnam, however. Conflicts in the United States caused American soldiers in Vietnam to turn on each other in frustration. The black fighter, according to Terry:

> fought at a time when his sisters and brothers were fighting and dying at home for equal rights and greater opportunities, for a color-blind nation promised to him in the Constitution he swore to defend. He fought at a time when some of his leaders chastised him for waging war against a people of color, and when his Communist foe appealed to him to take up arms instead against the forces of racism in America. The loyalty of the black [soldier] stood a greater test on the battleground than did the loyalty of any other American soldier in Vietnam. . . .

*The military was fully integrated by the Vietnam War in the 1960s and '70s. However, the growing Civil Rights movement at home and the American public's opposition to the war put great pressure on African-American soldiers.*

Still, the black soldiers fought hard and well. One officer related, "Two or three of the NVAs [soldiers in the North Vietnamese Army] I interrogated told me they knew when black soldiers were in action, because they would throw everything they could get their hands on—grenades, tear gas, anything. They feared the black soldier more than the white soldier because the black soldier fought more fiercely, with more abandonment."

When the war ended, American veterans of all races returned to a bitter, hostile nation. The less-than-friendly welcome home was even more frustrating for African-American veterans, who once again were subjected to racial prejudice. As Richard J. Ford III described in *Bloods*, "You know, they decorated me in Vietnam. Two Bronze Stars . . . I was wounded three times. The officers, the generals, and whoever came out to the hospital to see you. They respected you and pat you on the back. They said, 'You brave. And you courageous. You America's finest. America's best.' Back in the States the same officers that pat me on the back wouldn't even speak to me."

Two decades later, 100,000 African-American men and women were among the American military personnel in the Persian Gulf as part of Operation Desert Storm. They performed in the spirit of the proud, black fighting men who made up the Buffalo Soldiers.

The story of the Buffalo Soldiers offers one of the best examples of honor, courage, and perseverance in the face of adversity. As William Leckie explains in *The Buffalo Soldiers*:

> The experiment with Negro troopers launched in 1866 proved a success by any standard other than that of racial prejudice. By 1891 the combat record spoke for itself. They had fought on the plains of Kansas and in Indian Territory, in the vast expanse of West Texas and along hundreds of miles of the Rio Grande and in Mexico, in the deserts and mountains of New Mexico and Arizona, in Colorado and finally in the rugged grandeur

of the Dakotas. Few regiments could match the length and sweep of these activities. . . .

Their labors were not limited to the battlefield. They built or renovated dozens of posts, strung thousands of miles of wire, and escorted stages, trains, cattle herds, railroad crews, and surveying parties. Civil officials, particularly in Texas and New Mexico, could not have performed their duties without them. Their scouts and patrols opened new roads, mapped vast areas of uncharted country, and pinpointed for oncoming settlers the location of life-giving water. . . .

Prejudice was an ever-present obstacle and often hampered their effectiveness. Trouble with civilians in the tough little frontier towns was frequent. . . . In the last analysis, however, the records reveal a simple fact. The Ninth and Tenth Cavalry were first-rate regiments and major forces in promoting peace and advancing civilization along America's last continental frontier. The thriving cities and towns, the fertile fields, and the natural beauty of that once wild land are monuments enough for any buffalo soldier.

While few would disagree with Leckie's overall assessment of the Buffalo Soldiers, many felt the men had not been shown the proper acknowledgment and respect. One of those who believed that a greater tribute was due the Buffalo Soldiers was General Colin Powell, the first black chairman of the Joint Chiefs of Staff.

In the early 1980s, Powell, who had risen through the army ranks to deputy commanding general, was assigned to Fort Leavenworth, Kansas. This was the spot where the 10th Cavalry had been formed more than a century before. While searching for a barbershop in downtown Fort Leavenworth, Powell came across one owned by a man who called himself "Old Sarge." When Powell asked the man's name, he answered, "Jalester Linton, 10th Cavalry, Buffalo Soldier."

Powell recalls feeling he was shaking the hand of black history. He and Linton discussed sites on the military post that had been named for famed fighting

*General Colin Powell, the first African American to chair the Joint Chiefs of Staff, credited the Buffalo Soldiers for creating opportunity in America's military for people of all races.*

men, places such as Grant Avenue and Eisenhower Hall. When Powell asked Linton if there was any such tribute to the Buffalo Soldiers, Linton replied, "Well, there's Ninth and Tenth Cavalry Avenues."

After that meeting, Powell became curious about the history of the Buffalo Soldiers. He wrote:

> I started reading everything I could lay my hands on. What I learned filled me with pride at the feats these black men had achieved and with sadness at the injustices and neglect they had suffered.
>
> Blacks had fought in just about all of America's wars. They served to prove themselves the equal of white soldiers, which was precisely why some whites did not want blacks in a uniform.
>
> For twenty-two years . . . Colonel Benjamin H. Grierson commanded . . . the Tenth Cavalry. When Grierson finally bade goodbye to his troops, he said, 'The valuable service to their country cannot fail, sooner or later, to meet with due recognition and reward.' Ninety-five years later, it was too late for reward, and I did not see much recognition of the Buffalo Soldiers either.

One day, while jogging past the Fort Leavenworth post cemetery, Powell reached an old, empty trailer park. His eyes lit upon two crooked, decrepit old signs —one at Ninth Cavalry Avenue and one at Tenth Cavalry Avenue. Powell, upset by what he had seen, contacted Robert von Schlemmer, a retired colonel who served as post historian. "Is that the best we can do?" Powell inquired. "Two dirt roads in an abandoned trailer park?"

Recalling other military memorials, Powell envisioned a statue honoring the black soldiers "on the bluff overlooking the Missouri [River], with the cavalry man facing west, headed toward the future." Feeling "a duty to those black troops who had eased my way," Powell made the Buffalo Soldiers memorial a personal crusade. He assigned Captain Phil Coker, a white member of the 10th Cavalry, which had been integrated during the Korean War, to the project.

"You're going to immortalize your old outfit," Powell told Coker. "You're going to dig up the history of the Buffalo Soldiers."

"Coker went at it as if we were talking about *his* ancestors," Powell recounts in his autobiography. "He scoured the archives while I started looking for money. Those troops had suffered second-class treatment after serving as first-class fighting men. I was determined that the Buffalo Soldiers were finally going to go first-class."

When Powell left Fort Leavenworth, he asked Alonzo Dougherty, an Army civilian official, to keep the project alive. Dougherty made some progress, but lacked the funding to complete the memorial. Then a black naval officer, Commander Carlton Philpot, came to Fort Leavenworth to teach at the Command and General Staff College and fell in love with the idea of a Buffalo Soldiers memorial. Philpot was not content with a statue of a soldier on horseback. He wanted a small park with a reflecting pool and the statue.

At Powell's urging, wealthy *TV Guide* publisher and philanthropist Walter Annenberg promised $250,000 if Powell could raise a matching sum. Powell secured funding from some other philanthropists as well as family members of former Buffalo Soldiers. On July 28, 1990, ground was broken for the memorial in the place where the black cavalrymen had once stood. Powell writes:

> The stars that day were Sergeant Major William Harrington and First Sergeant Elisha Kearse, both ninety-five years old, authentic Buffalo Soldiers who had served long ago in all-black regiments. As I shook their gnarled hands, I felt connected to my past, to Lieutenant Flipper, and to blacks who fought on the Western plains and charged up San Juan Hill, all but invisible to history. As we drove the ceremonial shovels into the ground, the story of those two old soldiers was a hole in history about to be filled.

On that day, Powell spoke to some 2,000 people who had gathered for the ceremony, and the first black

*On July 25, 1992, the Buffalo Soldier Monument was dedicated at Fort Leavenworth. Over 100 years after the black cavalry troops were formed, their role in shaping America's frontier and contributing to the growth of the U.S. military is finally being recognized.*

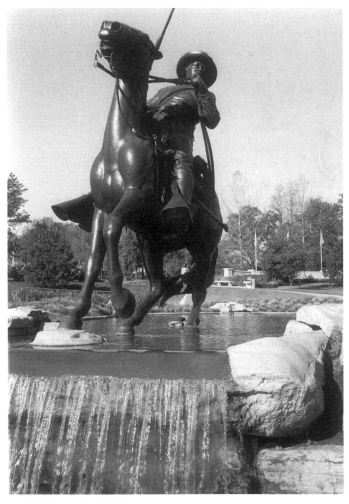

chairman of the Joint Chiefs of Staff acknowledged his debt to the Buffalo Soldiers.

On July 25, 1992, the Buffalo Soldier Monument was dedicated at Fort Leavenworth. The monument, designed by architect Tom Kolarik, includes a tiered fountain topped with a sculpture of a Buffalo Soldier on horseback. Eddie Dixon, an African-American artist, created the sculpture. On one side of the monument is a plaque for the 9th Cavalry; on the other side, a plaque for the 10th.

General Powell attended the dedication ceremony, which drew a crowd of 12,000. At least two Buffalo

Soldiers were present, Sergeants Harrington and Kearse.

President Clinton visited with four Buffalo Soldiers at the White House in December 1993. Trooper James Madison, Sergeant Harrington, Sergeant Mark Matthews, and Trooper Frederick Williams wore their Buffalo Soldier hats proudly as they were photographed with the president.

Acknowledgment of the Buffalo Soldiers' contributions continues to grow. In April 1994, the U.S. Postal Service issued a commemorative Buffalo Soldier stamp. The citizens of Leavenworth, Kansas, are working to create a Buffalo Soldier museum.

In 1992, the Soldiers in Blue Buffalo Soldiers Program was developed by A. C. Jackson and Kenneth Pollard of the Texas Parks and Wildlife Department. The program teaches people of all ages about little-known African-American history through historical reenactments, drills, a junior Buffalo Soldier summer reading program, and special outreach to young people in urban areas. The Soldiers in Blue are bringing history to life with the mission of helping minority youths to feel pride in themselves and their history and to feel a renewed sense of hope for their future.

In a recent one-year period, some 70,000 people of all ages attended the Soldiers in Blue programs. The legacy of dignity, bravery, and courage left by the men named in honor of the sacred animal of the plains continues to inspire people of many races and from all walks of life.

The words of African-American author John Killens deftly capture the essence of the bold fighting men who struggled mightily on so many fronts: "When the battle is won, let history be able to say to each one of us: he was a dedicated patriot. Dignity was his country. Manhood was his government and Freedom was his land."

# Chronology

1770    Former slave Crispus Attucks is killed in the "Boston Massacre" on March 5.

1776    On January 16, the U.S. Continental Congress decides to enlist free black men in the army. Some 7,000 African Americans fight for America's freedom between 1776 and 1781.

1812–  African-American soldiers and sailors serve in the fight against British
1814     troops in the War of 1812.

1862    The U.S. Congress allows black men to enlist in the Union Army during the Civil War. By the end of the struggle, 186,000 African Americans serve in the Union Army, and over 33,000 are killed.

1866    An act of Congress forms the 9th and 10th Cavalries and the 38th, 39th, 40th, and 41st infantry regiments to serve in the U.S. Army during peacetime.

1867    The 9th and 10th Cavalries go West to end the Indian Wars, earning the nickname "Buffalo Soldiers."

1869    An act of Congress combines the 38th, 39th, 40th, and 41st infantry units into the 24th and 25th Infantry Divisions.

1870    Emmanuel Stance becomes the first of 20 Buffalo Soldiers to receive the Congressional Medal of Honor for bravery in battle.

1872    John H. Conyers becomes the first black man admitted to the U.S. Naval Academy.

1875    The Ninth Cavalry is called to hunt for the renegade Apache Chief Victorio.

1877    Lieutenant Henry O. Flipper becomes the first African American to graduate from West Point and the first African-American officer of the 10th Cavalry.

1898    The Buffalo Soldiers are called to fight in the Spanish-American War in

Cuba and are instrumental in the American victory at San Juan Hill.

1914–
1918    Nearly 400,000 African Americans enter the armed forces during World War I. In 1918, Henry Johnson and Needham Roberts become the first Americans—and the first black men—to receive the *Croix de Guerre* (French Medal of Honor) for their valor in the First World War.

1936    Benjamin O. Davis Jr. becomes the first African American to graduate from West Point in the 20th century.

1940    Benjamin O. Davis Sr. is named the first black general in the regular army.

1941–
1945    Over a million African-American men and women serve in the U.S. Armed Forces during World War II.

1941    The Army Air Corps' 99th Pursuit Squadron becomes the first black unit of its kind. Colonel Benjamin O. Davis Jr. becomes commander of the 99th in 1942.

1948    On February 2, President Harry Truman signs Executive Order 9981, ordering an end to segregation in the U.S. Armed Forces.

1950–
1953    Soldiers of all races fight together in the Korean War. Segregated African-American fighting units are eliminated.

1965–
1975    Twenty African-American soldiers receive Congressional Medals of Honor for their outstanding service during the Vietnam War.

1971    Samuel L. Gravely is appointed the first black admiral in the U.S. Navy.

1975    Daniel "Chappie" James becomes the first African American to rise to the rank of four-star general.

1991–
1992    100,000 African-American men and women fight in the Persian Gulf War, known as "Operation Desert Storm."

1992    The Buffalo Soldier Monument, with sculpture by black artist Eddie Dixon, is dedicated on July 25 at Fort Leavenworth, Kansas.

# Further Reading

Bachrach, Deborah. *The Spanish-American War*. San Diego: Lucent Books, 1991.

Barbeau, Arthur E. and Henri, Florette. *The Unknown Soldiers: African-American Troops in World War I*. New York: Da Capo Press, 1996. (Originally published in 1974 in Philadelphia by Temple University Press.)

Cashin, Herscel V., et al. *Under Fire with the Tenth U.S. Cavalry*. New York: Arno Press and *The New York Times*, 1969.

Cox, Clinton. *The Forgotten Heroes: The Story of the Buffalo Soldiers*. New York: Scholastic, 1993.

Estell, Kenneth, ed. *Reference Library of Black America*. Detroit: Gale Research Inc., 1994.

Flair, Clay. *The Forgotten War: America in Korea*. New York: Times Books, 1987.

Hauser, Pierre. *The Community Builders 1877–1985*. New York/Philadelphia, Chelsea House Publishers, 1995.

Katz, William Loren. *The Black West*. Seattle: Open Hand Publishing, 1987.

Leckie, William H. *The Buffalo Soldiers: A Narrative of the Negro Cavalry in the West*. Oklahoma City: University of Oklahoma Press, 1967.

Milner, Clyde A. II, O'Connor, and Sandweiss. *The Oxford History of The American West*. New York/Oxford: Oxford University Press, 1994.

Powell, Colin, with Joseph E. Persico. *My American Journey*. New York: Ballantine Books, 1995.

Reef, Catherine. *Buffalo Soldiers*. New York: Twenty-First Century Books, 1993.

Terry, Wallace. *Bloods: An Oral History of the Vietnam War by Black Veterans.* New York: Bantam Books, 1984.

*Cobblestone, The History Magazine for Young People*, February 1995. Peterborough, New Hampshire: Cobblestone Publishing, Inc.

# INDEX

Alexander, John, 48
Annenberg, Walter, 93
Apache Indians, 25–26, 27, 31–37, 38
Arapaho Indians, 21, 22, 27
*Army and Navy Journal*, 14
Arthur, Chester A., 48
Attucks, Crispus, 10

Ballou, Charles C., 78
Barbeau, Arthur E., 74, 75, 79
Barber, Merritt, 47–48
Beauman, William, 18
Billy the Kid, 53
Black Coyote, 41
*Black Soldier, White Army*, 86
*Black West, The* (Katz), 9, 15, 54, 56
*Bloods: An Oral History of the Vietnam War by Black Veterans* (Terry), 87, 90
"Boomers," 57–60
*Buffalo Soldiers: A Narrative of the Negro Cavalry in the West, The* (Leckie), 33, 37, 38, 90
Buffalo Soldiers Memorial, 91–95
Buffalo Soldiers museum, 95
Bullis, John, 55, 56
Bush, George, 76
Bussey, Charles M., 85–86
Butler, Benjamin, 13

Carney, William, 13
Carpenter, Louis, 17
Cheyenne Indians, 21, 22–24, 27
Chief Victorio. *See* Victorio

Christy, William, 24
Civil rights movement, 87
Civil War, 11–14, 19
Clinton, Bill, 95
Coker, Phil, 92–93
Comanche Indians, 21, 23, 27, 55
Committee on Fair Employment Practice, 80
*Community Builders, The* (Hauser), 15
Congressional Medal of Honor, 13, 26, 36, 55, 67, 70, 76
Cooper, Charles, 52–53
Cox, Clinton, 22, 27, 28, 33, 41, 44
Crow Indians, 21

Davis, Benjamin O., Sr., 71, 79
Davis, Benjamin O., Jr., 79, 81–82
Davis, H. T., 18
Dixon, Eddie, 94
Dougherty, Alonzo, 93
Douglass, Lewis, 13
DuBois, W. E. B., 73
Dwyer, Molly, 47

Emancipation Proclamation, 12
Executive Order 8802, 80

54th Massachusetts Infantry regiment, 13
Flair, Clay, 85
Flipper, Henry O., 45–48, 93
Ford, Richard J., III, 90
*Forgotten Heroes: The Story of*

*the Buffalo Soldiers, The* (Cox), 22
*Forgotten War: America in Korea, The* (Flair), 85
Fort Concho, New Mexico, 44, 51, 53, 54
Fort Davis, Texas, 19, 47
40th Infantry, 9
41st Infantry, 9
Fort Leavenworth, Kansas, 14, 16, 19, 77, 91, 94
Fort Riley, Kansas, 19, 27

Geronimo (Apache chief), 31–32
Grant, Ulysses S., 12
Green, John E., 71
Grierson, Benjamin H., 14, 16–18, 19, 27, 36, 37, 38, 44, 51, 60, 92
Griffith, Thomas, 68

Harrington, William, 93, 95
Harrison, Benjamin, 60
Hatch, Edward, 14, 19, 32, 34, 35, 37, 59, 60
Hauser, Pierre, 15
Henri, Florette, 74, 75, 79
Henry, Boston, 44
Henry, Guy, 26
Hoffman, William, 16, 17, 18
Holliday, Preston, 70–71
Hooker, Theodore, 34

Jackson, A. C., 95
Jackson, Andrew, 55
Johnson, Henry, 76
Johnson, John, 11
Jordan, George, 21, 36, 60
*Journal of Negro History*, 11

Kansas Pacific Railroad, 23, 27
Katz, William Loren, 9, 15, 54, 56
Kean, William B., 86
Kearse, Elisha, 93, 95
Kibbett, John (Seminole chief), 55
Killens, John, 95
King, Irsle, 48
Kiowa-Apache Indians, 27
Kiowa Indians, 21, 23, 27
Knox, Frank, 69
Kolarik, Tom, 94
Korean War, 85–86, 92

Lakota Indians, 21, 23, 38–41
Leckie, William, 32–33, 37, 38, 51, 90, 91
Lincoln, Abraham, 9
Lincoln, New Mexico, 53–54
Linton, Jalester, 91–92
Lynch, John R., 71
Lynchings, 44

McCarthy, Tom, 44
McClain, Henry, 60
MacColl, Ray, 48
Madison, James, 95
Matthews, Mark, 95
Miles, Nelson A., 40, 41
Military Academy, U.S., 45, 46, 48, 49, 81
Miller, Dorie, 81
Momeyer, William, 81
Moutcastle, John W., 86
My American Journey (Powell), 45, 93
Myers, Walter Dean, 11

National Association for the

Advancement of Colored People (NAACP), 74, 79, 80, 81, 83
Native Americans, 21–41, 44, 54–57. See also individual tribes
9th Colored Cavalry, 9, 14, 19, 44, 53–54, 57–60, 85, 91, 94
and Chief Victorio, 32–37
and Indian Wars, 21–22, 24, 25, 26, 29
and the Lakota Indians, 38, 40
and Spanish-American War, 66, 67–69
and World War I, 77
92nd Infantry Division, 73, 76, 83, 85
93rd Infantry Division, 73, 75, 76, 78, 83, 85
99th Pursuit Squadron, 79, 81–82
Now Is Your Time! The African American Struggle for Freedom (Myers), 11

Officer Candidate Schools, 79
Officer Training School, 74
Oklahoma Indian Territory, 57–60
Operation Desert Storm. See Persian Gulf War

Payne, David L., 58, 59
Perry, B. F., 43
Pershing, John J., 48, 68–69, 74
Persian Gulf War, 90

Phillips, Joseph, 55
Philpot, Carlton, 93
Pollard, Kenneth, 95
Powell, Colin, 45, 49, 71, 91–95
Prioleau, George, 71
Pullen, Frank W., 65–66
Purington, George, 53

Racism, 19, 22, 27, 43–49, 57, 66, 75, 76, 78–79, 80, 82, 83, 86, 88, 90, 91. See also Segregation
Revolutionary War, 10, 11
Roberts, Filmore, 28
Roberts, Thomas A., 78–79
Robinson, Elmer E., 77
Roosevelt, Franklin D., 80–81
Roosevelt, Theodore, 67, 70, 71
Rough Riders, 67, 68, 70–71

Salem, Peter, 10
San Juan Hill, Battle of, 67–69, 93
Segregation, 43, 44, 70, 73, 74, 76–77, 78–81, 83, 86–87, 92
Seminole Negro Indian Scouts, 54–57
77th Combat Engineers Company, 85
Shafter, William, 47
Shaler, Nathan, 11
Shoshone Indians, 21
Sioux Indians. See Lakota Indians
Sitting Bull (Lakota chief), 39

# INDEX

Smith, E. L., 23
Soldiers in Blue Buffalo
    Soldiers Program, 95
*South to the Naktong, North to*
    *the Yalu,* 86
Spanish-American War, 48,
    63–70, 71, 73
Stance, Emanuel, 25–26
Stowers, Freddie, 76

10th Colored Cavalry, 9, 14,
    16–18, 44, 45, 48, 52–53,
    54, 60, 85, 91, 92, 94
    and Chief Victorio, 36–38
    and Indian Wars, 21,
    23–24, 26, 27, 29
    and Spanish-American
    War, 66, 67–69, 70
    and World War I, 77
Terry, Wallace, 87, 89
38th Infantry, 9

39th Infantry, 9
332nd Fighter Group, 81
369th Infantry, 75–76
Truman, Harry S., 83
24th Infantry, 66, 69, 85–87
25th Infantry, 65, 66, 69, 85

United States Army Distin-
    guished Flying Cross
    (DFC), 76
*Unknown Soldiers: African-*
    *American Troops in World*
    *War I, The* (Barbeau and
    Henri), 74
Urban League, 74, 79, 80

Victorio (Apache chief),
    31–37, 46, 47
Vietnam War, 87–90
Villa, Pancho, 49
von Schlemmer, Robert, 92

Wally, Augustus, 67
War of 1812, 11
Watkins, William, 44
Weasel Bear, Louise, 41
West Point. *See* Military
    Academy, U.S.
White, Horton, 85
Whittaker, Johnson C., 45
Wilks, Jacob, 22
Williams, Frederick, 95
Williams, George Washing-
    ton, 21
Woodward, Samuel, 19
World War I, 49, 73–77, 78,
    79
World War II, 69, 77, 79–83
Wounded Knee, massacre at,
    40–41

Young, Charles, 48–49, 71

# PICTURE CREDITS

page

2    Courtesy Frederic Remington Art Museum, Ogdensburg, NY

8    Schomburg Center for Research in Black Culture, New York Public Library

10    Library of Congress, #62-2141

12    (left) Library of Congress, #62-415A; (right) Library of Congress

15    The National Archives, neg. #111SC130526

16–17    Library of Congress, #B8184

20    Institute of Texan Cultures, University of Texas

23    The Kansas State Historical Society, Topeka

24–25    Institute of Texan Cultures, courtesy Mrs. Annie R. Lee, San Antonio, Texas

26    Library of Congress, photo courtesy of Mike McClure, Ethete, Wyoming

30    Smithsonian Institution

32    Schomburg Center for Research in Black Culture, New York Public Library

35    Corbis-Bettmann

39    South Dakota State Historical Society, Pierre, South Dakota

40    Corbis-Bettmann

42    Courtesy of the New-York Historical Society, New York City, neg. #48099

45    Schomburg Center for Research in Black Culture, New York Public Library, U.S. Military Academy Archives

46    Copyright Texas Memorial Museum

49    Corbis-Bettmann

50    Photo by Ben Wittick, courtesy Museum of New Mexico, neg. #50887

54    Courtesy William Loren Katz, The Black West, Simon & Schuster, Touchstone Edition

56    Courtesy William Loren Katz, The Black West, Simon & Schuster, Touchstone Edition

57    Western History Collections, University of Oklahoma, Phillips Collection #2056

59    Library of Congress

62–63    The National Archives, neg. #111SC84821

64    Corbis-Bettmann

66    Corbis-Bettmann

68    The National Archives, neg. #111SC90108

72    Corbis-Bettmann

75    Corbis-Bettmann

77    Corbis-Bettmann

78    Schomburg Center for Research in Black Culture, New York Public Library

80    (left) The National Archives, neg. #54-3482; (right) The National Archives, neg. #111SC192258

82    Corbis-Bettmann

84    Corbis-Bettmann

87    The National Archives, neg. #111SC353469

88    Schomburg Center for Research in Black Culture, New York Public Library

89    Corbis-Bettmann

92    Corbis-Bettmann

94    Courtesy Fort Leavenworth, Public Affairs Office

TARESSA STOVALL is the co-author of *Catching Good Health*, a guide to homeopathic medicine, and she has worked as a speechwriter for U.S. Secretary of Health and Human Services Louis W. Sullivan, as media coordinator for the Children's Defense Fund–Black Community Crusade for Children, and as executive director of the National Association of Minority Media Executives. A native of Seattle, Washington, TaRessa lives in the Washington, D.C., area with her husband and two children.